The Southern Bed and Breakfast Book

Corinne Madden Ross
Revised by:
Patricia G. Sabiston

The East Woods Press
Charlotte, North Carolina

Copyright 1981, 1984, 1985 by Fast & McMillan Publishers, Inc.

All rights reserved. No part of this book may be reproduced without permission from the publisher, except by a reviewer who may quote brief passages in a review; nor may any part of this book be reproduced, stored in a retrieval system or transmitted in any form or by any means, electronic, mechanical, photocopying, recording or other, without permission from the publisher.

Library of Congress Cataloging in Publication Data

Ross, Corinne Madden.
   The Southern Bed and Breakfast Book.

   Rev. ed. of: The Southern Guest House Book. 2nd rev. ed. 1984.
   Includes index.
   1. Bed and breakfast accommodations — Southern States — Directories.
I. Sabiston, Patricia G. II. Ross, Corinne Madden. Southern Guest House Book.
III. Title
TX907.R589   647'.947503   85-45690
ISBN 0-88742-062-1 (pbk.)

Cover design by Talmadge Moose
Inside illustrations and photographs provided by the guest houses of the South
Printed in the United States of America

East Woods Press Books
Fast & McMillan Publishers, Inc.
429 East Boulevard
Charlotte, NC 28203

Contents

Map to Guest Houses vi

Introduction 9

Alabama 13
   Northern Alabama 14
      Mentone 15
      Scottsboro 17
      Birmingham 19
   Central Alabama 19
      Montgomery/Auburn 19
   Southern Alabama 22
      Mobile 22

Florida 25
   Florida's East Coast 26
      Fernandina Beach/Amelia Island 26
      St. Augustine 29
   Southern Florida 34
      Key West 35
   Florida's West Coast 38
      Sarasota/Tarpon Springs 38

Georgia 41
   The Atlanta Area 42
   Georgia's Northeast Mountains 44
      Lakemont/Mountain City/Clarkesville 44
   The Classic South 48
      Augusta 48
   The Heart of Georgia 49
      Senoia/Macon 49
   Plains Country 51
      Columbus 51
   The Colonial Coast 52
      Savannah/Statesboro 52

Bed & Breakfast

- Louisiana 63
  - North Louisiana 64
    - Ruston 64
  - Acadiana 66
    - Baton Rouge/St. Francisville/New Iberia 66
  - New Orleans 71

- Mississippi 79
  - Southern Mississippi 80
    - Natchez/Lorman 80
  - Central Mississippi 88
    - Vicksburg/Port Gibson 88
  - Northern Mississippi 92
    - Holly Springs 92

- North Carolina 95
  - Coastal Region 97
    - The Outer Banks 97
    - Kill Devil Hills/Ocracoke 97
    - New Bern/Edenton 101
    - Wilmington 103
  - The Piedmont (Midlands) Region 105
    - Raleigh/Greensboro/Winston-Salem 105
    - Pinehurst 110
    - Charlotte 111
  - North Carolina's Mountains 114
    - Boone 115
    - Blowing Rock 116
    - Asheville/Hendersonville/Lake Lure/Tryon 118
    - Cherokee/Bryson City/Franklin/Glenville 124

- South Carolina 129
  - The Low Country 130
    - Charleston 131
    - Beaufort 139

- Tennessee 143
  - West Tennessee 144
    - Memphis 144
  - Middle Tennessee 146
    - Nashville/Murfreesboro 146
  - East Tennessee 147
    - Gatlinburg/Chattanooga/Knoxville 147
    - Kingsport/Rogersville 149

Contents

Virginia and Washington, D.C. 151
  Northeastern Virginia 152
    Washington, D.C. 152
    Arlington/Alexandria/Fredericksburg/Orange 156
  Tidewater Region 159
    Richmond 159
    Jamestown/Mathews/Williamsburg/Yorktown 161
    Hampton/Newport News/Norfolk/
      Portsmouth/Virginia Beach 165
  The Eastern Shore 167
    Assateague and Chincoteague Islands 168
  Virginia's Mountains 170
    The Shenandoah Valley/Winchester/Mt. Jackson 170
    Upperville/Middleburg/Sperryville 171
    Skyline Drive/Charlottesville 176
    The Blue Ridge Parkway and Virginia's Highlands 178
    Lexington/Warm Springs/Hot Springs 178
    Lynchburg 182

Index 185

Southern Guest Houses

All cities and towns shown have one or more bed-and-breakfasts.

Washington, D.C.
Middleburg
Upperville
Mt. Jackson
Sperryville
Orange
Warm Springs
Charlottesville
Chincoteague
Hot Springs
Lexington
Richmond
Mathews
Lynchburg
Williamsburg
Virginia Beach
Virginia
Edenton
Kill Devil Hills
Greensboro
Winston-Salem
Raleigh
Boone
Blowing Rock
North Carolina
Knoxville
Asheville
Lake Lure
Hendersonville
New Bern
Ocracoke
Bryson City
Tryon
Charlotte
Pinehurst
Glenville
Franklin
Wilmington
Lakemont/
Mountain City
South Carolina
Clarkesville
Hoschton
Atlanta
Augusta
Charleston
Senoia
Beaufort
Macon
Statesboro
Savannah
Columbus
Georgia
Fernandina Beach (Amelia Island)
Florida
St. Augustine
Winter Park
Palm Harbor
Tarpon Springs
Sarasota
Miami
Key West
Marathon

Introduction

One of the most romantic regions of our nation is the American South. Steeped in history, each area is distinctive in its tradition, food and people. Sections that were devastated during the Civil War have at last recovered, with a dynamic upsurge of energy and enterprise evidenced in the South's booming industry and flourishing agriculture. It is a vibrant, vital region boasting an amazing diversity of scenery, all manner of outdoor activities and sports, and a wealth of art, music and festivals.

Yet respect for history and tradition is strong, and the grandeur of the past has been lovingly preserved. The traveler can still find and enjoy the Classic South—the scent of magnolias, magnificent antebellum plantation homes framed by live oaks festooned with Spanish moss, glorious azalea gardens, and historic towns and cities where a slower, gentler way of life still exists. And the best way to discover the atmosphere and the attractions, both old and new, in this region is to plan your trip around some of the South's delightful bed-and-breakfast guest houses.

If you have never stayed in one, you may be wondering what a bed and breakfast is, and what it has to offer. With a few exceptions, it is a private home with several rooms available for guests, and it provides breakfast, either included in the rates or for a modest fee. In Europe and Great Britain, this homey form of overnight lodging has long been popular. In America, bed and breakfasts were few and hard to find until the 1970s; they were, in fact, a well-kept secret shared only by experienced travelers and those fortunate enough to come upon them by chance. Today, happily, the number of bed and breakfasts in America is increasing dramatically.

This book describes unique bed-and-breakfast establishments located in Alabama, Florida, Georgia, Louisiana, Mississippi, North Carolina, South Carolina, Tennessee, Virginia and Washington, D.C. Also included are descriptions and some history of the various states and regions, and tips on places to see and things to do.

Note that guest house rates, once extremely economical, are now as varied as the services and ambiance found at each bed-and-breakfast guest house. As a rule, bed and breakfasts are located in or near a town, so that visitors can easily walk to restaurants, shops,

Bed & Breakfast

historic sites and other local points of interest. Men or women traveling alone will find them a safe and pleasurable alternative to other forms of lodging, and they are ideal for families. Most owners welcome children, and there is almost always a spacious yard or porch where youngsters can play. (Each entry includes information about any restrictions for children.)

The greatest charm of guest houses, however, lies in their surprising individuality. In the South, their range of architectural styles is as diverse as the region itself. Southern guest houses include stately eighteenth- and nineteenth-century mansions with cool, secluded courtyards; white-columned plantation homes surrounded by extensive grounds; handsome, storied townhouses; rambling beach cottages or country farmhouses, and even contemporary mountain chalets. Many offer a luxurious, old-world elegance seldom found elsewhere today; others are merely ordinary homes providing clean, simple surroundings. A great many Southern bed and breakfasts are historic buildings; a number are listed in the National Register of Historic Landmarks and are included on house tours in their locales.

Many guest houses are furnished with lovely antiques; some have rooms with fireplaces. A number of houses offer entire suites, with sitting rooms and fully equipped kitchens. A pleasant parlor or lounge is usually available for guests, sometimes with a cheerful fire blazing away in chilly weather. Books, magazines, games and television are often provided, too, for rainy days or evening entertainment. Some thoughtful hosts place fresh flowers or complimentary wine and fruit in each room; others serve afternoon tea or sherry to their guests. Breakfast may be served on a shady terrace, in a cozy kitchen, or perhaps in a splendid, formal dining room.

Bed-and-breakfast owners are as individual as their homes; they include grandmotherly ladies, young couples and older ones, families, and single men and women of all ages. The majority share one agreeable characteristic—they truly enjoy their guests and often form lasting friendships with them. You may, of course, have as much privacy as you wish. But do try to spend some time with your hosts and fellow guests; you'll find them interesting, congenial people. Many proprietors also act as concierges, making dinner reservations for guests at local restaurants or arranging tours of the area. Personal service and gracious extra touches are the keynotes of bed-and-breakfast hospitality.

As the houses are generally small, with only a few guest rooms, making reservations in advance by phone or letter is a good idea, and sometimes required. Some owners also request an advance deposit; a few ask for a minimum stay of two or three days, especially over holiday weekends. Credit cards are not usually accepted (although exceptions have been noted at the end of some guest house entries); cash or traveler's checks are preferred. Personal checks, too, are often acceptable, but it is advisable to ask ahead of

Introduction

time. The rates for each house (for double occupancy) are listed under one of four general categories:

Inexpensive	($10–$25)
Moderate	($25–$45)
Moderately Expensive	($45–$65)
Expensive	($65– up)

Most bed-and-breakfast houses stay open year-round; some may close in the off season or for a brief holiday. Information on dates open has been included for each house.

The descriptions of the houses included are as accurate as possible. Sometimes, however, situations or owners change after the book has gone to press. If you should find any of the accommodations not measuring up to your expectations, I will very much appreciate your letting me know so that we can reevaluate the listing for the next edition. It should also be mentioned that the guest house experience is not for everyone; not all of the houses offer private baths, and most do not provide a private phone or television set for each room. Some travelers do not enjoy sharing breakfast with strangers. Few, however, find any of these particulars an inconvenience. Several guest house owners, in their turn, have requested that I add a note on "proper etiquette" for visitors! They ask that guests show concern for others in the matters of noise and privacy; do not bring pets along if the house does not accept them; do not allow children to run around unaccompanied or expect baby-sitting service if it is not offered, and do not request special items for breakfast unless absolutely necessary.

If you are as curious about people and places as I am, and delight in staying in some of our country's most beautiful and historic homes, you will find the bed-and-breakfast guest homes of the South exactly your cup of tea. Discovering the joys of guest house travel, in fact, may well turn out to be the highlight of your vacation! Your hosts and hostesses will welcome you with genuine warmth and interest — and with the South's outstanding lure, a generous sampling of its fabled hospitality.

Alabama

Alabama, with its astonishing diversity of scenery and attractions, promises a wealth of surprises for travelers. The state's topography ranges from the rolling foothills and peaks of the Appalachians in the northeast to flat, coastal plains and the white sand beaches of the Gulf of Mexico. Still predominantly agricultural, Alabama also contains several large cities including Birmingham, one of the South's major industrial centers. The state's historic sites span an impressive range of time, from Indian battlegrounds to Confederate shrines and the country's first space center.

Alabama's northern region includes mountain meadows, clear lakes, covered bridges, waterfalls, awesome canyons and—believe it or not—a ski resort! Central Alabama, called "The Cradle of the Confederacy," has the historic city of Montgomery, the oldest recorded caverns in America and a number of elegant Greek Revival mansions. Southern Alabama, much of which curves around scenic Mobile Bay, offers the city of Mobile with its well-preserved collection of Old South architecture, a winery and fabulous seafood.

The state's lakes, mountains and seashore provide super swimming, hiking, hunting and fishing; its cities boast fine museums, zoos and an array of cultural activities and entertainment. There are old forts and shrimping villages to explore and colorful festivals to attend, and in the spring, lovely gardens bloom with spectacular displays of camellias, magnolias and azaleas.

The oldest historic sites in Alabama are its Stone Age caverns and Indian mounds. Indians gave the state its name: *alabama* means "clearers of land." In the early 1500s Spanish seamen sailed along the coastline; in 1540 Hernando de Soto and a party of soldiers seeking fabled cities of gold marched through the region. Their custom of looting and burning villages along the way caused understandable resentment among the Indians, who fought back in a series of fierce but generally unsuccessful skirmishes. At the battle of Mauvila, near Choctaw Bluff, some 11,000 Indians were said to have been killed. De Soto, who was wounded in the fray, continued his march and ended up a year later at the Mississippi River, where he died.

Although Spain made several attempts to colonize Alabama's coast, no lasting Spanish settlement was ever established. In the mid-1600s,

Bed & Breakfast

England also laid claim to the region but did nothing with it. Toward the end of the seventeenth century, the French explorer Robert Cavelier, Sieur de La Salle, followed the Mississippi River southward to its mouth and claimed the vast territory, which he named Louisiana, for France. King Louis XIV sent Pierre Lemoyne, Sieur de Iberville, to establish a French settlement on the Gulf Coast near Biloxi, Mississippi, in 1699. Iberville's brother, Jean Baptiste Lemoyne, Sieur de Bienville, was appointed governor of the Louisiana territory in 1702 and moved the seat of government to what is now Mobile, Alabama. France ceded most of the region to England in 1763; twenty years later England gave the southern part of the territory to Spain. Spain ceded all but a small portion to the United States, which later took over the remaining Spanish land as part of the Louisiana Purchase.

In 1861, at the start of the Civil War, Alabama was the fourth state to secede from the Union, and Montgomery served as the Confederate capital for several months. Jefferson Davis was inaugurated there as president of the Confederacy, and it was from Montgomery that the fateful order was sent to fire on Fort Sumter. Although few Civil War engagements took place on Alabama soil, Mobile Bay was the scene of a notable battle in 1864. Admiral David Farragut's armada of seventeen ships was making its way into the bay to fire on Fort Morgan when the *Tecumseh,* vanguard of the fleet, hit an underwater mine (called a torpedo in those days) planted by the Confederates. The ship sank in minutes, but the Union admiral was undaunted and from his ship, the *Hartford,* cried out the famous words: "Damn the torpedoes. Full speed ahead." While Union troops attacked from land, Farragut and his remaining ships bombarded the fort. The blockade won the battle; after eighteen days Fort Morgan surrendered.

During the Reconstruction period following the war, Alabama suffered greatly from political corruption and dissension. But by the late 1800s the state's iron and steel industry, centered in Birmingham, began to grow, and Alabama started on the path to recovery. In this century the Tennessee Valley Authority built massive dams along Alabama's section of the Tennessee River, turning once-flooded land into fertile soil and providing vast resources of inexpensive electric power. Today the state's principal industries include lumbering and food processing. Although Alabama is nicknamed "The Cotton State," cotton is no longer a major crop. Much of the rich central region known as the Black Belt, where once grew the cotton that brought great wealth to nineteenth-century planters, has been converted into grazing pastures for cattle.

Northern Alabama

In Florence, in the western part of the region, travelers may visit

Alabama

the log cabin birthplace of W. C. Handy, "Father of the Blues," and the Indian Mound Museum. The mound is the largest on the Tennessee River; the museum, which displays paintings and slides showing various periods of the mound builders' culture, contains artifacts dating back 10,000 years. Not far away, in Tuscumbia, is Ivy Green, Helen Keller's childhood home. On Friday nights during July and August *The Miracle Worker* is performed on the grounds, which also include the pump where Anne Sullivan spelled out the word *w-a-t-e-r* into young Helen's hand. Another intriguing site in the area is the Key Underwood Memorial Park Coon Dog Cemetery, just south of Cherokee.

Over to the east in Huntsville, the Alabama Space and Rocket Center allows visitors to experience the sights and sounds of space and view the rocket that carried man to the moon. Northeast of Huntsville, near Bridgeport, Russell Cave National Monument offers fascinating demonstrations of prehistoric man's weapons and tools; Sequoyah Caverns to the south are noted for their crystalline reflecting lakes and rainbow falls. Cloudmont, a ski resort, is nearby in Mentone. At DeSoto State Park in Fort Payne, 110-foot waterfalls cascade with a roar into a rock basin, and Little River Canyon, one of the deepest gorges east of the Rockies, has sheer rock walls rising 700 feet in some places.

In Anniston, to the south, the Museum of Natural History displays a large collection of birds and a reconstructed flying dinosaur. Fort McClellan, a major Army basic training center, includes the U.S. Women's Army Corps Museum and the Military Police Museum. For a superb view of the region, head south from Anniston to Cheaha Mountain, at 2407 feet above sea level the highest point in Alabama. Northwest, near Oneonta, the 200-foot-long Horton Mill Covered Bridge stands 70 feet above the Black Warrior River. Nearby Horse Pens holds a number of bluegrass festivals and crafts fairs on spring and fall weekends.

Mentone

Mentone, in scenic northeastern Alabama near the Georgia border, has been a popular mountain retreat since the late 1800s. According to local history, a New Yorker named John Mason set out to test the climate and waters in various parts of the country "hoping to find a place that would restore his body to its former healthy state." While staying in a nearby town, Mason was told about the health-giving properties of the area's mineral springs; he found accommodations with a family on Lookout Mountain and discovered that his health did improve. In 1872, Mason moved his family to Mentone permanently. His son, Ed Mason, bought a tract of land at Vernons Gap and, while studying surveying in college, began to lay out the future town. Other homebuilders began to come to the mountain, and in 1884,

Bed & Breakfast

Dr. Frank Caldwell built the Mentone Springs Hotel for travelers.

Today Mentone, which means "a singing stream," is a year-round resort. In May, Lookout Mountain blooms with rhododendrons and day lilies; in July the town hosts a well-attended arts and crafts festival. Autumn brings glorious fall colors; the last week of October is highlighted by the Fall Color Fest, with hayrides, apple bobbing, pumpkin carving, ghost tales, German food and a grand Halloween costume ball at the old hotel. Grass skiing in summer and snow skiing in winter are available at Cloudmont.

The Mentone Inn. Set atop beautiful Lookout Mountain, the rustic inn was built in 1927 in traditional American style and was operated as the DeSoto Lodge for nearly fifty years. Amelia Kirk-Brooks purchased the lodge in 1975; after renovating the property and returning the structure to its original 1920s style, Ms. Kirk-Brooks once again opened the lodge to guests as Mentone Inn.

The inn's handsome interiors are all tongue-and-groove, clear-grain pine from Mississippi; for guests there are twelve rooms, each with its own bath. In addition, there is a three-bedroom cottage with baths, sitting room and porch. Most of the individually decorated rooms include iron beds; the bathrooms boast claw-foot tubs. For relaxing, living rooms with comfortable sofas and chairs include color TV, and the large front porch is a grand place to read, rock, play cards or put jigsaw puzzles together. The view, with layer after layer of mountains and valleys, is especially fine at sunset time. There are hot tubs for luxurious soaking, and for game players the inn offers horseshoes, badminton and volleyball.

Alabama

Breakfast, included in the rates, varies but may include homemade waffles, fresh fruit and juices in season, quiches, Southern breakfast omelet and crepes along with coffee or tea. Your hostess may also, on request, provide other meals. Ms. Kirk-Brooks will be pleased to recommend restaurants and shops in the area; some are within walking distance. Mentone has a number of excellent antique shops, and history buffs will like St. Joseph's on the Mountain, right next door to the inn. The oldest structure in the town, the church was originally a simple log cabin. In Fort Payne, twelve miles away, you can attend theatrical events at the old opera house, and the annual June Jam features the renowned country music group Alabama in concert. DeSoto State Park offers hiking, tennis courts and a pool; DeSoto Falls has river swimming and canoeing. The region also includes two excellent golf courses and Sequoyah Caverns.

The Mentone Inn, P.O. Box 284, Mentone, AL 35984; (205) 634-4836 after April 15; before April 15 call (205) 634-4108. (When you make your reservations, you will be sent a map with directions.) Rates are moderate, lower for stays of two weeks or more. Children are welcome, but your hostess prefers that younger children stay in the cottage. No pets, please. Parking is available. Open April–Dec. 1.

Scottsboro

About halfway between Mentone and Huntsville, Scottsboro is famed for First Monday, a century-old observation of barter day. Held on the first Monday of each month on Courthouse Square in the center of the historic district, First Monday was originated by a group of merchants as a horse- and mule-swapping day. Over the years First Monday has grown into a lively festival, with banjo and fiddle music accompanying the bartering of all manner of items. You'll find everything from handmade quilts and homemade bread to axe handles and antiques. The Tennessee River, a few miles away, provides all manner of water sports, and a nineteen-hole championship golf course is easily accessible.

The Brunton House Bed and Breakfast. Norman and Jerry Brunton are your friendly hosts at their comfortable bungalow-type home in Scottsboro. The house, built in the mid-1920s, is painted Williamsburg blue and trimmed with oyster and rustic red. According to Jerry Brunton, additions to the structure have been made several times over the years. The original sections of the house boast 10-foot, 10-inch ceilings. Lovely pine floors have been carpeted for protection.

There is an attractive, spacious living room just for guests, with a fireplace, color TV and a ceiling surrounded by ornate wooden molding; the room is white with pale green trim. Just off the living room is the Music Room, bright and sunny and decorated in blues

Bed & Breakfast

and greens. The downstairs guest bedrooms include an interior room with pretty pink and green flowered wallpaper, located in the middle of the house and especially popular as it is very quiet and cool in summer and warm in winter; the cheerful Sun Room, across the hall from a full bath; the Yellow Room, with maple furniture and a half bath, and the pleasant Blue Room, featuring soft blue wallpaper with tiny white flowers.

Upstairs, the Bruntons offer a cozy semi-efficiency with an iris-wallpapered bedroom and private bath. Your hosts' own quarters include a spacious "great room," originally the office for the old cotton warehouse next door. The decor is charmingly English, with rough plaster walls, dark-beamed ceiling and a fireplace; the floors are carpeted in red. Here the Bruntons entertain their guests, and also serve breakfast. Out of doors, a large, shaded back yard provides space for children to play or picnics.

Jerry Brunton says her husband is an excellent cook who loves to prepare breakfast, and the meal—included in the rates—consists of juice, eggs, bacon or sausage, toast and coffee or tea. If requested, the Bruntons will provide evening meals, complete with wine, for an extra fee. The house is only two blocks from downtown Scottsboro, where there is a variety of restaurants and shops.

The Brunton House Bed and Breakfast, 112 College Ave., Scottsboro, AL 35768; (205) 259-1298. (Just half a block off Broad Street, Scottsboro's main street.) Rates are moderate, lower for longer stays, for families and for senior citizens (10% discount). Well-behaved children are welcome; no pets please. Smoking is permitted in the living room only. Parking is available out front. Open year-round.

Brunton's Bed and Breakfast. Norman and Jerry Brunton also operate a bed-and-breakfast referral service which offers host homes in Alabama and Tennessee, plus listings in a number of other Southern states. In Alabama their accommodations, mainly in the north and central regions, include a century-old farmhouse on a 128-acre farm in Falkville; a late-nineteenth-century house in the historic section of Old Decatur; a 10-acre hideaway on Sand Mountain, overlooking the Tennessee River; pleasant suburban homes in Scottsboro, Athens and Tuscaloosa, and many more. Breakfast is included in the rates; the meal may be a continental breakfast of juice, coffee and rolls or toast or—in some instances—a full Southern breakfast.

Contact: Brunton's Bed and Breakfast, P.O. Box 1066, Scottsboro, AL 35768; (205) 259-1298. You will be sent a Host Directory and a reservation form. Send back the filled-in form with your check for the total amount due for your visit, plus appropriate tax. Rates are inexpensive to moderate. You will be given the name and address of the host home you have chosen, and you may communicate with your hosts directly. Brunton's Bed and Breakfast also provides maps and brochures about the area you will be visiting, along with confirmation of your reservation.

Alabama

Birmingham

Named after the manufacturing city in England, Birmingham was founded in 1870. The region's rich deposits of iron, coal, limestone and other ores soon turned the city into the industrial center of the South. Tannehill Historical State Park, where Birmingham's iron industry began, is built around the ruins of the pre–Civil War Tannehill Furnaces. Destroyed by Union troops during the war, the wooded ruins have been restored and are open to the public. The park also includes an old gristmill and cotton gin, authentic pioneer homes and other interesting structures. The downtown area of the city has recently undergone a major renaissance and, now called Birmingham Green, offers tree-shaded walkways, flowers and attractive shops and restaurants. The city's Museum of Art contains a remarkable collection of Wedgwood as well as Remington bronzes and the famed Kress Collection of Renaissance art. Visitors will also enjoy a tour of the Botanical Gardens and the Birmingham Zoo. Looming over the city from atop Red Mountain is the imposing figure of Vulcan, Roman god of fire and metalworking. The largest iron statue ever cast, Vulcan stands fifty-five feet high and weighs sixty tons, and may be ascended for a grand overall view of Birmingham.

Bed & Breakfast Birmingham, Inc. Ruth Taylor manages Bed & Breakfast Birmingham, a reservation service with some fifty host families. Her listings cover the greater Birmingham area and include a number of historic older homes, as well as several elegant suburban homes with pools. One host raises miniature horses and, according to Ms. Taylor, "bakes the most wonderful cream puffs!" All of the accommodations have been personally inspected.

Contact: Bed & Breakfast Birmingham, Inc. P.O. Box 31328, Birmingham, AL 35222; (205) 591-6406. You will receive a reservation form to fill out and return with a deposit; Ms. Taylor will arrange suitable accommodations to fit your needs. To avoid disappointment, as much advance notice as possible is requested; reservations for families may require extra time. No pets, please. Rates range from moderate to expensive and include continental breakfast. The advance deposit is refundable, less a modest cancellation fee, up to 7 days before the reservation date.

Central Alabama
Montgomery/Auburn

Central Alabama is a wonderfully historic region; through it runs the Black Belt, a thirty-mile-wide strip of rich black soil. Proud ante-bellum mansions, once the center of great plantations, still

Bed & Breakfast

stand; pecan, magnolia and ancient oak trees grace the landscape. In the attractive capital city of Montgomery, the State Capitol building, completed in 1851, may be toured. Nearby is the First White House of the Confederacy, dating to 1835. A two-story white frame house, the building was briefly lived in by Confederate President Jefferson Davis and now contains period furnishings and Davis family memorabilia. The Governor's Mansion, a Greek Revival structure built in 1908, is also open to the public.

Other historic Montgomery sites include the 1855 Rice-Semple-Haardt House, comprising several architectural styles and containing a small museum with memorabilia of Lurleen Wallace, Alabama's only woman governor; the Dexter Avenue King Memorial Baptist Church, where the late Rev. Martin Luther King, Jr., was pastor; and the Ordeman-Shaw Complex, with an 1850 Italianate townhouse, a Greek Revival cottage, an old log cabin and other structures. Jasmine Hill Garden, about eight miles north of the city, features a reproduction of the ruined Greek Temple of Hera, as well as lovely flowers and blooming shrubs.

The Tuskegee Institute National Historic Site, a short drive west from Montgomery, includes the George Washington Carver Museum. Carver, who was born in slavery, joined the institute at the request of its founder, Booker T. Washington. During his long lifetime of teaching and research, Carver developed more than 300 by-products from the lowly peanut and some 50 from the sweet potato. Eufala, to the southeast, is worth a side trip to see its collection of stately old mansions.

Horseshoe Bend National Military Park, northeast of Montgomery near Dadeville, was the scene of a great battle between the Creek Indians and Gen. Andrew Jackson's army in 1814; a three-mile tour road offers living history demonstrations. Some of the Creeks, a band called the "Red Sticks," had earlier attacked Fort Mims. In retaliation, U.S. military troops struck back and General Jackson's Tennessee Militia won a decisive victory over the Indians at the Horseshoe Bend of the Tallapoosa River.

Near Childersburg, to the northwest, DeSoto Caverns, the birthplace of the Creek Nation and America's oldest recorded caves, may be explored. The site was sacred to the Creeks; after their defeat at Horseshoe Bend the surviving Red Sticks retreated there, but their ancient home was no longer a refuge. Along with the rest of the Creek Nation, they were soon removed to Oklahoma so that the land could be opened to settlers. Selma, a port city on the Alabama River west of Montgomery, includes several classic mansions including Sturdivant Hall, said to be haunted by the ghost of John Parkman, a prominent banker whose career ended in disgrace and imprisonment. Farther west, in Demopolis, magnificent Gaineswood was the focal point of a large Black Belt plantation from 1821 until the Civil War.

Just northeast of Montgomery, off Interstate 85, is the quaint university town of Auburn. The historic district has several dwellings of Civil War significance. During the Depression, the university had only a three-member administration. Today, it is highly respected and "electric" during sports seasons. Only twenty miles away is Victory Land race track, and Callaway Gardens (in Georgia) is about an hour's drive.

The Crenshaw Guest House. This wedgwood blue, graceful Victorian home was built in 1890 by Auburn University professor Bolling Hall Crenshaw. Delicate gingerbread trim enhances the charm, and bay windows overlook an acre of giant oak and pecan trees. As fourth-generation Auburn residents, your hosts, Fran and Peppi Verma, have a wealth of knowledge about the area you will be visiting. Fran will be glad to assist in obtaining meeting facilities, office and travel services, information on various parts of town and real estate services available. To enhance the atmosphere of the house, the Vermas have borrowed old Auburn souvenirs from area residents to display throughout the house.

The two roomy suites are located on the ground floor and display a unique blend of nineteenth-century charm and modern convenience. Amid period decor, guests will enjoy cable TV, a parlor, and a private telephone and bath. The Carriage House is located behind the main building and has a double bed on the first floor, plus additional sleeping space in the loft. The Carriage House has a private bath, wet bar and refrigerator. Guests are also invited to enjoy the large, screened back porch which overlooks the garden.

In addition to a fresh fruit basket upon arrival, guests will enjoy the sumptuous, complimentary breakfast featuring specialty breads, fresh fruits, assorted cheeses, coffee or tea, juice, milk, cereal and yogurt. Breakfast is delivered daily to each suite or may be enjoyed on the back porch.

The house is only five blocks from downtown Auburn and the main

Bed & Breakfast

campus gates, five blocks from Jordan-Hare Football Stadium; obviously it is convenient for students and parents. The Vermas also plan to cater to the needs of business people and newcomers to the area.

The Crenshaw House, 371 N. College St., Auburn, AL 36830; (205) 821-1131. (From Montgomery, take Exit 51 off I-85 and follow S. College until it becomes N. College.) Rates range from moderate to moderately expensive; American Express, Visa and MasterCard are accepted. Children may be accommodated in the Carriage House only. No pets, please. Parking available. Open year-round.

Southern Alabama

Mobile

Most of Southern Alabama's attractions are centered on Mobile Bay, on the Gulf of Mexico. The city of Mobile celebrates Mardi Gras each February with parades, fancy dress balls and other exciting events. Founded in 1711 by Jean Baptiste Lemoyne, Sieur de Bienville, Mobile is proud of the fact that its Mardi Gras is the oldest in the United States. From late February to early April, the city's magnificent azaleas are celebrated in the Azalea Trail Festival, with a variety of entertainment and self-guided tours of the marked thirty-five-mile route.

Mobile includes four historic districts: Church Street, DeTonti Square, Oakleigh Garden and Old Dauphin Way, each of which offers a fascinating array of architectural styles. Beautiful ante-bellum Oakleigh stands among venerable live oaks on a section of an old Spanish land grant; the Richards-DAR House, circa 1860, is a restored townhouse in the Italianate style; Carlen House, built in 1842, is a superb example of Creole Cottage architecture, a style which developed during French Colonial times. The Museum of the City of Mobile, on Government Street (which is lined with handsome old houses), contains a host of interesting items pertaining to the city's history, plus Mardi Gras costumes and a large collection of Boehm porcelain. In Langan Park, on Museum Drive, you'll find the very attractive Fine Arts Museum of the South. A gem of a small museum, its collections include paintings from the seventeenth century to the present, Southern furniture, ethnic art and contemporary crafts.

Fort Conde, a reconstructed French fort dating to the early 1700s, is great fun to visit. Guards in authentic French period costumes demonstrate the workings of cannons and muskets, and there is a small village with shops. Another Mobile site especially appealing to youngsters is the U.S.S. *Alabama* Battleship Memorial Park on the bay. The park includes the *Alabama*, a submarine, tanks, planes and helicopters.

Alabama

Vincent-Doan Home. Built in 1827, the Vincent-Doan home is the oldest house in Mobile and the only known example of French Creole architecture in the city. Originally built by Capt. Benjamin Vincent, a prosperous sea captain, the home has gone through extensive architectural changes over the years. Your hostess, Ms. Betty Mann Doan, has a printed history of the house available for guests to read. The home is listed on the National Register of Historic Places. There

are three guest rooms, all on upper floors. One has a private bath and two share a bath. Guests are invited to use the living room and sitting room, which has a TV. In addition to a welcoming beverage, a complimentary, full Southern country breakfast is provided. Guests are only fifteen minutes from Bellingrath Gardens, ten minutes from Battleship Park, and thirty minutes away from the dock to go deep-sea fishing.

Vincent-Doan Home, 1664 Springhill Ave., Mobile, AL 36604-1405; (205) 433-7121. (Write for directions.) Rates are moderate, with discounts for longer stays and senior citizens. Visa and MasterCard are accepted. Children and pets are welcome. Parking available at the house. Open year-round.

Alabama's most famous gardens—Bellingrath—are located twenty miles southwest of Mobile, near Theodore. Particularly lovely in the spring when some 250,000 azalea plants are at their peak of color, the gardens offer special flowers for each season of the year. The 800-acre estate includes several types of terrain, a bird sanctuary and the Bellingrath home; there's a restaurant on the grounds, too. The house, which is open to the public, contains antiques, fine china and the world's largest collection of Boehm porcelain.

Heading south from Mobile, you'll come to Bayou la Batre, a quaint French fishing village where the Blessing of the Shrimp Fleet is held

Bed & Breakfast

each year on the last Sunday in July. Dauphin Island, just off the coast, is the site of pre-Civil War Fort Gaines and a Confederate museum. During the Civil War, on Aug. 5, 1964, Admiral Farragut's fleet faced crossfire from both Fort Gaines and Fort Morgan; the Union forces later captured the forts and blockaded the port of Mobile. Fort Morgan, around on the eastern side of Mobile Bay at Gulf Shores, lies at the end of a narrow strip of land extending into the bay.

Also on the east side of Mobile Bay is Malbis, a Greek community founded in 1906, with the splendid Byzantine Malbis Greek Orthodox Church. To the north, take the Perdido-Rabun Exit from I-65 to the Perdido Vineyards. Tours of the winery are available throughout the year, with complimentary wine tasting. Visitors may purchase wines with names like "Magnolia" or "Rose Cou Rouge" (which translates loosely into "Redneck Rose") and, in the summer, pick grapes straight from the vine. In Enterprise, over near Dothan to the east, fanciers of oddities will find the Boll Weevil Monument, the only monument ever erected to an insect pest

Florida

Florida ... the name conjures up visions of golden beaches, suntanned bodies, and palm trees rattling in balmy sea breezes. Although the state has its share of ante-bellum mansions and Civil War history, Florida is not "Southern" in the traditional sense. It is more like a separate world—a water-world, with 8426 miles of tidal coastline, a wealth of crystal springs, 30,000 lakes, and great, brooding swamps. It is Walt Disney World, too, and the launching ground for the world of outer space.

More than four and a half centuries ago the Spanish navigator Juan Ponce de Leon landed on the east coast not far from present-day St. Augustine. In those days, Spanish adventurers made many expeditions into the wilderness of the New World looking for gold (which they often found) and for mythical cities or other wondrous fancies (which they did not). Ponce de Leon was searching for a fabled island which legend claimed held a Fountain of Youth. To the lasting regret of everyone over forty, he failed in his mission. He did, however, discover Florida.

Recognizing a good thing when he saw it, Ponce de Leon claimed the new territory for Spain. Perhaps because he landed during the Easter season *(Pascua de Flores,* the Feast of Flowers), he named the region *La Florida.* In 1521, having received permission from King Ferdinand V of Spain to colonize the new territory, Ponce de Leon returned. He attempted to establish a settlement on Florida's west coast, but the colony was attacked by Indians, and Ponce de Leon was severely wounded. He and his followers fled to Cuba, where he subsequently died. Hernando de Soto and other Spanish explorers also visited Florida in the ensuing years, but hostile natives prevented any further colonization for some four decades.

The arrival in 1564 of French Huguenots, who came to found a settlement near the mouth of the St. Johns River, began a lengthy period of back-and-forth struggles for sovereignty of the territory. King Philip II of Spain sent a force to wipe out the French; the French went after the Spanish in revenge. Spain, triumphant for the moment, set up missions in Florida; then the English entered the picture. Sir Francis Drake burned St. Augustine in 1586, and English pirates terrorized the coast in the 1600s.

In the early 1700s, English colonists from Carolina burned St.

Bed & Breakfast

Augustine again, but the Spanish held on. Pensacola, the region's second Spanish colony, was later briefly captured by the French. In 1763 Spain gave Florida to England in exchange for Cuba; in 1783 Spain got Florida back again, in return for the Bahamas. Twelve years later, Spain sold West Florida (which included the land west of the Apalachicola River plus the southernmost parts of what are now Alabama, Mississippi and Louisiana) to France. The United States purchased West Florida as part of the Louisiana Purchase in 1803. During the War of 1812, Spanish Florida caused the United States a great deal of trouble. Criminals took refuge across its border, Seminole Indians made frequent raids into Georgia, and the Spanish allowed British troops to occupy Pensacola. At the same time, the Spanish rulers were plagued by American settlers in West Florida. In 1821, the Spanish government gave up the region for good, ceding it to the United States in exchange for $5 million.

American settlers immediately began to pour into the new territory; to accommodate them the U.S. government took over much of the land belonging to the Seminoles. For some twenty years bloody battles raged between the Indians and the U.S. military. Most of the Indians who survived were persuaded to move west—all the way to Oklahoma. Florida became a state in 1845 and hoisted its first state flag, a multi-striped design which bore the testy demand: "Let Us Alone." Sixteen years later Florida seceded from the Union, but grudgingly rejoined the United States once again in 1868. The postwar years were hard ones for Florida; in the latter part of the 1800s and in the early 1900s, however, conditions began to improve. Part of the Everglades was drained, creating new vegetable-growing land, and cities and winter resorts sprang up along the coasts. In the 1920s a fantastic land boom developed, only to crash under the weight of the Depression and several deadly hurricanes. Since then, Florida has been on an unprecedentedly stable upswing, based on tourism and new industry.

Florida's East Coast

Starting in the north, travelers exploring the east coast of Florida will find famous old shore resorts including Fernandina Beach; Jacksonville, the state's commercial hub; and the charming 400-year-old city of St. Augustine. Continuing south, coastal highlights include twenty-three-mile-long Daytona Beach and the Kennedy Space Center on Cape Canaveral. Farther south are West Palm Beach, Fort Lauderdale and Miami.

Fernandina Beach, Amelia Island

Amelia Island boasts an unusual distinction. It is the only region

Florida

in the country to have existed under eight different flags: French, Spanish, English, Patriots, Green Cross of Florida, Mexican, Confederate and United States. Fernandina, once a haven for pirates and smugglers and later a major shipping port, is now a quiet community with uncrowded beaches, a thirty-block historic district and a picturesque shrimp fleet. Fort Clinch State Park is located here, and on the first weekend of May each year the town holds "The Isle of Eight Flags" Shrimp Festival presenting art and crafts shows, a mock pirates' landing and the Blessing of the Shrimp Fleet.

The Bailey House. An 1895 Victorian home, with broad porches and a widow's walk, the Bailey House is listed on the National Register of Historic Places and is located in the heart of a thirty-block historic district. You can walk to the downtown stores, restaurants, the marina and the shrimp docks. A prime example of Queen Anne architecture, the elegant bed-and-breakfast inn includes Tiffany-style stained-glass windows, six fireplaces, and heart-pine floors, woodwork and staircase.

George W. Barber of Knoxville, Tennessee, was the architect. With its multiple turrets, gables, bay windows and fish-scale decorations, the house took three years to build, at the then impressive cost of $10,000. (Most of the houses of that time cost approximately $1,500.)

It was the first house in Fernandina Beach to have a built-in icebox (still intact), plumbing and electricity.

Today, the Bailey House is owned by Tom and Diane Hay. They have four upstairs rooms for guests, each with a private bath. Downstairs there is a reception hall with a magnificent fireplace and a formal dining room where a continental breakfast is served between

Bed & Breakfast

8 and 9 a.m. (included in the rate). The Bailey House offers the use of bicycles and beach towels, and for year-round comfort, the house has central heat and air.

The Bailey House, 28 S. 7th St. (P.O. Box 805), Fernandina Beach, FL 32034; (904) 261-5390. (From I-95, east on A1A (8th Street) to Center Street. Turn left, then left again at 7th Street (1 block). The house is at the corner of 7th and Ash streets.) Rates are moderately expensive to expensive. (Special weekly rates are available.) American Express is accepted. Children over 10 are welcome. No pets, please. No smoking allowed except on the veranda. Parking available. Open year-round.

The 1735 House. In 1735, James Edward Oglethorpe, then governor of Georgia, sailed southward on an expedition and discovered a barrier island off the northeast coast of Florida. Ignoring the fact that the region belonged to Spain, Oglethorpe claimed the island for England and named it Amelia for Princess Amelia, young sister of King George II. The 1735 House was named in honor of that historic visit.

A white frame structure with black shutters, the house is set in a superb location right on Amelia Island's thirteen-mile stretch of beach. The owners, David and Susan Caples, believe that it is the only bed-and-breakfast establishment on Florida's east coast that directly overlooks the Atlantic Ocean. They offer guests five double rooms and a suite with two bedrooms and a living area. Three of the rooms are on the ground floor. Wicker or rattan furnishings are used in all the living/entertainment areas, antiques and collectibles in the bedrooms. All of the accommodations include private baths. Guests may also stay in a lighthouse! The round, four-story building was built about eight years ago as a private home. It has two bedrooms, a living/kitchen area, an observation deck and a working light on top. Popular with honeymooners, it accommodates up to four people.

Breakfast, included in the rates, consists of juice, fresh fruit and homebaked pastries, coffee or tea. It's delivered to your room in a wicker basket, along with the morning paper. The town of Fernandina Beach is approximately two miles away, so you will need a car to reach restaurants and shops.

The 1735 House, 584 S. Fletcher (Rte. A1A), Amelia Island, FL 32034; (904) 261-5878. (Take I-95 to Yulee exit near the Florida/Georgia border; proceed east on Rte. A1A approximately 15 miles to Amelia Island.) Rates are expensive, lower from November to February, and there is a 10% discount for 1-week stays. American Express, MasterCard and Visa are accepted. No children or pets, please. There is parking at the house. Open year-round.

St. Augustine

With its ornate wrought-iron gates and balconies, red-tiled roofs and cobblestone streets, Spanish Colonial architecture and horsedrawn carriages, St. Augustine instantly transports the visitor back in time. And so it should: it is the oldest city in the United States. Some years after Ponce de Leon explored Florida, Spain's King Philip II sent Don Pedro Menendez de Aviles to the region to drive out French settlers. Menendez arrived in 1565, led the raid, and set up the small colony of St. Augustine as a Spanish military outpost.

To consolidate Spanish possession of the territory, the awesome Castillo de San Marcos was contructed in the late 1600s. Indian laborers took twenty-five years to complete its grim ramparts, dungeons and massive walls. (Some of the walls are thirteen feet thick.) The fortress withstood countless attacks and sieges; in later years it served as a British and then an American military prison. Castillo de San Marcos is now operated by the National Park Service. Several times a day visitors can watch the firing of one of the fort's old cannons, a seemingly high-risk process carried out by a person lighting a frayed rope on the end of a very long stick. The flaming rod is then poked gingerly into the cannon as the firer hastily moves to one side.

The flags of Spain, England, the Confederacy and the United States have all flown over St. Augustine. The town, burned and pillaged several times, has miraculously survived with an amazing number of its historical features intact. The Oldest House, dating to the early 1700s, represents several different periods; its site has been in constant use since the early 1600s. The present house, which includes many additions, is constructed of coquina, a limestone formed of broken shells and coral. The floors are tapia, a mixture of lime, sand and oyster shell.

One of the most interesting sections of the city is San Augustin Antigua, a re-creation of the original eighteenth-century Spanish village. Restored and reconstructed houses and other buildings, with overhanging balconies and hidden walled gardens, line the narrow

Bed & Breakfast

byways. Costumed artisans demonstrate their crafts—weaving, baking, candle dipping, silversmithing and the like—in a number of exhibit buildings. St. George Street extends the length of the restoration area, from the old City Gate to the Plaza de la Constitucion with its handsome statue of Ponce de Leon. At the Visitor Information Center near the City Gate, visitors can view a movie about St. Augustine's more than 400 years of history and pick up all sorts of descriptive material. A leisurely walking tour is recommended, or you may choose a sightseeing train or horsedrawn carriage.

Casa de Solana. In 1763, Don Mañuel Solana, a Spanish military man, built Casa de Solana on the Matanzas Bay, the fourteenth oldest house in St. Augustine's historical district. An island unto itself, the inn is surrounded by a high wall with a grassy yard and miniature field inside the compound. There are four antique-filled guest rooms (two on the ground floor with private baths). All of them are suites, some with fireplaces and others with balconies. Jim and Faye McMurry have taken great pains to maintain the flavor of the Spanish period: thick coquina-shell walls, high ceilings with dark, hand-hewn beams and hand-pegged floors. All trim is painted "haint blue," an old Southern custom that is supposed to ward off evil spirits.

Travelers are always busy trying to take in all the sights of St. Augustine, so Faye has made certain that breakfast is a "peak experience" offering eggs, grits, homemade fruit-nut bread with molds of butter, fresh fruits, juice and coffee. This fare is included in the rates along with a morning newspaper, chocolates, a decanter of sherry and the use of bicycles for touring. Transportation is offered to some of the better restaurants that are not within walking distance.

Casa de Solana, 21 Aviles St., St. Augustine, FL 32084; (904) 824-3555. (Aviles Street is located between St. George Street and Charlotte Street, between US-1 S. and Matanzas Bay.) Rates are expensive, with lower rates for weekly stays. American Express, Visa and MasterCard are accepted. Children are welcome; no pets, please. Parking arranged by your hosts. Open year-round.

Florida

The St. Francis Inn. This remarkable guest house, which has been welcoming travelers continuously for 138 years, was built in 1791 as a home for Senor Gaspar Garcia. It is constructed of coquina, the same material used in the Oldest House, the Castillo de San Marcos and other historic buildings in St. Augustine. Between 1795 and 1838 the property changed hands numerous times; in 1838 it was purchased by Col. Thomas Henry Dummett, an Englishman and native of Barbados.

Dummett had been a wealthy landowner and sugar planter until a slave uprising forced him and his family to flee from Barbados to Florida. After the colonel's death in 1839 his family stayed on; in 1845 his widow, Mary, gave the house to her daughters, Anna and Sarah. Anna began operating the place as a boarding house, called "Miss Dummitt's" in a guidebook of the day. Another guide, pub-

lished in 1870, recommended the house most highly as furnishing excellent, pleasant accommodations for tourists "at about half the price of the hotels."

In the 1880s the house changed hands again, and the building was enlarged with the addition of a third story. New owners in 1925 installed central heating, bathrooms and a lavatory in each room. In 1948 the property was sold once more, and its name was changed to the St. Francis Inn. Today, Mr. and Mrs. Joseph F. Finnegan, Jr., own the house, and Marie Register is manager.

During the past few years the inn has been restored and refurbished. Air conditioning and many beautiful antiques and period pieces were added, and today it is a classic example of Old World Spanish architecture and charm. Every room has a fireplace, but no telephone or TV. Guests may watch TV downstairs in the old-fashioned parlor or enjoy games and the player piano.

Eleven guest rooms are available; two rooms and the cottage are on the ground floor. All rooms have private baths, and the five-room

Bed & Breakfast

cottage (the former slave quarters) has two bathrooms, two bedrooms, a kitchen, a living room and a Florida room. Included in the rates is a light breakfast of coffee, juice or milk; doughnuts or special breads; and apple butter or jam.

Entry to the house is through a courtyard and garden, containing jasmine, bougainvillea, banana trees and other tropical trees and plants. There is even a splashing fountain, and behind a wall, a pool and poolside patio. Guests may also enjoy relaxing on the balcony. The St. Francis Inn is located in the historic section of the city within a short walking distance of the Oldest House and many of St. Augustine's other sites of interest, including the waterfront. There are plenty of good restaurants nearby.

The St. Francis Inn, 279 St. George St., St. Augustine, FL 32084; (904) 824-6068. (Corner of St. George and St. Francis streets, 2 blocks south of the Town Plaza.) Rates range from inexpensive to expensive; special rates for longer stays. Children are welcome; no pets, please. Parking available on a private lot. Open year-round.

The Kenwood Inn. Early records show that the Kenwood Inn has played host to travelers for over a century. Built between 1865 and 1885, the inn has been extensively remodeled and restored by its present owners, Dick and Judy Smith. The rooms are decorated in themes representing different periods and styles of the past, ranging from the simple Shaker and country rooms to the more formal Colonial and Victorian rooms. There are fifteen rooms, six on the ground floor, and all have private baths. Guests are welcome to use the large living room with piano and fireplace as well as a TV room on the sun porch.

The Smiths offer friendly conversation over a delicious continental breakfast of home-cooked cakes or breads, fruit or juice and coffee. Breakfast is included in the rates.

Located within the historic district between the Oldest House and the famous Castillo de San Marcos, the Kenwood is within walking distance of many fine restaurants and all historic sights. The Intracoastal Waterway and beautiful beaches are nearby.

Florida

The Kenwood Inn, 38 Marine St., St. Augustine, FL 32084; (904) 824-2116. Rates are moderately expensive. Visa and MasterCard are accepted. Children over 6 are welcome; no pets, please. On-street parking only. Open year-round.

Westcott House. This fine example of vernacular architecture was built in the late 1880s by Dr. John Westcott. Perhaps best known for his interest in transportation, Dr. Westcott's more popular achievements included the Intracoastal Waterway linking the St. Johns River to Miami and the St. Johns Railroad, with tracks from the San Sebastian River to Tocoi. Your hosts, Ruth and Fredrick Erminelli, have retained the true image of past elegance in the Westcott House. The home has been completely renovated and is elaborately furnished with American and European antiques. The rooms have been modernized with queen- and king-size beds, telephones, cable TV, and year-round climate control. Eight guest rooms are available, three on the ground floor, and all have private baths. The home overlooks the beautiful Matanzas Bay, and guests may enjoy the view from the spacious veranda and courtyard. The living room is also a popular gathering place. A complimentary continental breakfast is served in the courtyard, Victorian porch or in the seclusion of your room. Also included in the rates is a bottle of wine upon arrival. At night, there's a complimentary turn-down service with chocolates adorning your pillows, a snifter of brandy by the bed and a luxurious terry-cloth robe for your bath. Since the house is located in the heart of the historic district, activities are varied.

Westcott House, 146 Avenida Menendez, St. Augustine, FL 32084; (904) 824-4301. (Write for brochure, which includes a full map.) Rates are expen-

Bed & Breakfast

sive, with special rates for longer stays. Visa and MasterCard are accepted. No children or pets, please. Your hosts request no smoking in the rooms. Only on-street parking available. Open year-round.

Central Florida

Central Florida's attractions range from the Ocala National Forest in the north to Lake Okeechobee just northwest of Palm Beach. The region is dotted with lakes; Okeechobee is the state's largest—a 530-square-mile fishing hole known for its largemouth bass. In between you'll find Silver Springs, where visitors can ride in glass-bottomed boats and take a jungle cruise past giraffes, camels and other exotic beasts roaming free on the banks of the Silver River, and Cypress Gardens. The Gardens, once a swamp, are now a lovely setting for water-ski shows, flowers, canals and rustic footbridges. The region also offers Walt Disney World, mecca to thousands of tourists each year. Disney's fabled Magic Kingdom is linked via monorail to the vast Epcot Center, which opened in 1982. Covering 260 acres, the complex includes Future World, with its gigantic globe housing Spaceship Earth, and World Showcase, which displays the architecture and culture of ten countries.

Southern Florida

Immense Everglades National Park sprawls for some 5000 square miles across Southern Florida. If you'd like to explore some of it, the eastern entrance is reached from Homestead, on Route 1 southwest of Miami. Turn west on Route 27 and drive 12 miles to the visitor center. Highway 27 is the park's main road and runs for 50 miles down to Flamingo. Half land, half water, the Everglades is a unique and magical region of mangroves, mahogany trees, dwarf cypresses, cabbage palms, wild orchids and ferns, and watery prairies of needle-sharp sawgrass. Wildlife (not immediately evident, but very much there) includes alligators, deer, bobcats, turtles, fish and birds in a multitude of varieties.

The Florida Keys begin farther south. Follow Route 1; the spectacular toll-free road, called the Overseas Highway, will take you all the way to Key West. The word *key* comes from the Spanish *cayo*, or cay, an offshore island of coral or sand. The Florida Keys consist of a 100-mile-long curving strand of some forty-two bridge-connected islands, plus a number of tiny islets and reefs. Pirates once used the Keys as a refuge and watering place; Indians found their way here to trade and occasionally to do battle. Several industries brought prosperity to the Keys for a time—cigar making, sponge gathering, and a local effort known as "wrecking" (salvaging wrecked ships and, it

Florida

is said, sometimes assuring profits by luring the ships onto the dangerous outer reefs). The U.S. Navy, brought in to rid the islands of pirates in 1822, stayed on and made Key West an important military base. Today the Keys' major businesses are tourism and fishing.

There is an elusive quality to the Keys: old-time inhabitants call it "a state of mind." Life on these remote islands is relaxed and easy-going, more Caribbean than it is American. The concerns of the mainland seem very far away. This highly individualistic world reflects a wide variety of tastes and cultures. Key West, for instance, was settled by a mixture of British, Cubans, Bahamians, Southerners and New Englanders. Key architecture ranges from charming Old World Spanish to contemporary tacky, with just about everything conceivable in between. Key cuisine is just as varied: you'll find Creole, Caribbean and Cuban specialties as well as barbecue and hushpuppies.

Collectors of the curious will be intrigued by the several "bat towers" located on the Keys, wooden structures that were built some years ago and stocked with bats from Texas. The idea was for the bats to devour the vicious local mosquitoes. Unfortunately, the notion did not work; the bats apparently preferred their own homegrown insects and immediately flew back to Texas.

At Key Largo, pay a visit to the Florida Keys Information Center. Helpful personnel will provide descriptive literature giving details on the Keys' many attractions and points of interest. Don't miss the John Pennecamp Coral Reef State Park nearby, a fascinating and extensive underwater park. You can explore the reef in a glass-bottomed boat, or skin or scuba dive for a close-up view of the brilliantly colored living coral and schools of tropical fish. Guides are available for tours. Farther down the chain of islands are Islamorada and Marathon, known for superb sportfishing. Big Pine Key offers thousands of exquisite orchids at the Summerland Orchid Gardens, and watchful visitors can spot rare white herons and the tiny Key deer.

Key West

Way down at the end of the Overseas Highway is Key West, southernmost city of the continental United States. (Island and city share the same name.) Native Key Westers are known as "conchs" (pronounced konks), named after the ubiquitous local shellfish. The best way to get your bearings is to take a ride on the Conch Tour Train, a 1½-hour narrated tour of the island. Then you can go off on your own, on foot or on rented bike or moped.

Artists and writers have long been attracted to the tranquil beauty of Key West; Ernest Hemingway's home is now a museum open to the public. A Spanish Colonial villa made of native stone, it sits behind a high brick wall amid masses of tropical trees and flowers.

Bed & Breakfast

Here and there and everywhere on the grounds (and inside the house) you will see cats, many of them double-toed. There are more than forty, all descendants of Hemingway's original fifty. Cat-loving visitors may, occasionally, adopt one of the kittens. They are free, but only if you promise to send a letter to the present owner of the house each year with a report on the animal's health and happiness.

Other interesting sites to be toured are the Audubon House (John J. Audubon's famed *Birds of America* is on display) and the Oldest House Museum (the Wrecker's House). Children will enjoy Flipper's Sea School, where Flipper and his dolphin family perform. At sunset, be sure to head for Old Mallory Square. Key West residents have made a ritual of gathering at the square at the end of the day to watch the impressive show as the flaming sun seems to plummet suddenly into the western sea. Key Westers are expert judges of their sunsets and award each, according to its merits, with an accolade of respectful applause or (if it is especially noteworthy) loud cheers!

Eaton Lodge. Surrounded by lush tropical greenery, century-old Eaton Lodge offers an open, airy ambiance. Owners Denison Tempel and Sam Maxwell operate the architecturally notable structure as "a traditional inn of distinction." For guests they have four double and three triple rooms, and two suites suitable for three to five persons. Each is individually decorated and has its own private bath. Five of the rooms are on the ground floor, several open onto air-cooled balconies, and others are located in the old coach house at the rear. A wealth of fine details such as paneled walls and polished wood floors have been enhanced by discreet modernization and the use of Designers Guild fabrics from England. Paddle ceiling fans are used throughout, combining with dual windows to take full advantage of Key West's breezes; air conditioning is also available.

A drawing room/parlor is available for guests' use, as is an inviting garden with orchids and palms. Winding pathways lead past a fish pond, around a coral rock-surrounded hot tub, and end at a secluded brick-paved terrace. A continental breakfast of fruit, fruit juice, coffee cake and coffee, included in the rates, is served in the garden. The white clapboard house is in the heart of Key West's Old Town, close to sightseeing activities and a large selection of excellent restaurants and shops. In addition to the area's nearby attractions, your hosts suggest a seaplane ride to the Dry Tortugas and a visit to Fort Jefferson, last in the chain of forts built during the Civil War.

Eaton Lodge, 511 Eaton St., Key West, FL 33040; (305) 294-3800. Your hosts will arrange airport pickup, if desired. Prices are expensive, lower from mid-May through November/early December and for weekly or longer stays. MasterCard and Visa are accepted. Well-behaved children are welcome; no pets, please. Parking is available at the house. Open year-round.

Curry House. This nineteenth-century Victorian "conch" house, a

Florida

typical Key West structure, is owned by Bobby and Dan (who prefer the informality of first names only). Large verandas, shuttered windows and doors, and country furnishings carry out the tropical island feel of the place. There is a common living room for guests to use and a garden with a Jacuzzi and a jungle pool. Accommodations include two rooms with shared baths and six with private baths, and two rooms are on the ground floor. A full breakfast of tropical French toast, banana-nut pancakes, ham, bacon, sausage and Key West omelets is included in the rates, and your hosts occasionally put on a barbecue for their guests.

Curry House, 806 Fleming St., Key West, FL 33040; (305) 294-6777. Rates are moderately expensive, lower May 1–Dec. 15 (except holidays) and for weekly summer stays. MasterCard and Visa are accepted. No children or pets, please. Parking is available. Open year-round.

Coconut Grove Guest House. Formerly known as the Jasmine Gypsy, this guest house is now owned by Berne Teeple, who says there have been considerable changes. The house caters primarily to the gay and lesbian crowd, although the general public is welcome. There are now fifteen guest rooms, two of which are suites. Six rooms are on the ground floor, and all have private baths.

The house is eighty years old and is a classic Victorian, complete with gingerbread trim and a widow's walk from which guests may enjoy a spectacular view of the sunset and the Gulf. Balconies are

filled with wicker furniture and hammocks. A pool is surrounded by lush vegetation. Special services include airport pickup, dinner reservations and snorkeling arrangements. Travelers are two blocks from the Gulf of Mexico and twelve blocks from the Atlantic Ocean. A complimentary continental breakfast is also provided.

The Coconut Grove Guest House, 817 Fleming St., Key West, FL 33040; (305)

Bed & Breakfast

296-5107. *Rates are moderately expensive, with special discounts for longer stays. American Express, Visa and MasterCard are accepted. No children or pets, please. No parking available. Open year-round.*

Florida's West Coast
Sarasota/Tarpon Springs

If you're a circus buff or have children along, you will want to visit Sarasota on the west coast of Florida. Once the winter home of the Ringling Brothers Circus, Sarasota today offers a cluster of circus-oriented museums including the impressive million-dollar Venetian-Gothic Ringling Residence. Farther north along the coast are St. Petersburg, where excellent beaches abound; Tampa, with its colorful Spanish/Italian section called Ybor City and Busch Gardens "Dark Continent" (a theme park and wild game preserve); and Tarpon Springs, famed for its sponge fishermen and Greek heritage. Weeki-Wachee to the north is another of Florida's many freshwater springs. Underwater performances of ballet, acrobatics, comedy and tableaux are presented daily in an auditorium that is itself built under water. The audience watches the show through thick plate glass windows. Tallahassee, the state capital, lies a shade inland on the northwest coast, and historic Pensacola is way over near the Alabama border. Both cities offer gracious touches of the Old South, and Pensacola includes a spicy dash of Spanish heritage going back to Colonial days.

A picturesque fishing village situated along Spring Bayou, Tarpon Springs is about twenty-one miles northwest of Tampa. In its heyday earlier in the century, the town was the center of the sponge fishing industry in the United States, with a fishing fleet of almost 200 vessels. Most of the sponge fishermen were Greek immigrants who brought with them their national customs and culture. Today, although the sponge industry is not as thriving as it was, Greek fishermen still go out to sea in their brightly decorated boats. And Tarpon Springs, with its colorful Greek ambiance, seems more like a small Mediterranean seaport than a typical Florida town.

Visitors can see the sponge boats along the seawall on Dodecanese Boulevard, and at the Sponge Docks explore the Spongeorama Exhibit Center where the history of the sponging industry is presented. St. Nicholas Greek Orthodox Cathedral is another highlight of the town with its neo-Byzantine architecture, icons, stained glass and sculptured marble. On Jan. 6 each year the Festival of Epiphany is held at the Cathedral, a brilliant spectacle that includes the blessing of the waters, the Diving for the Cross Ceremony, and a Byzantine choir.

B & B By the Sea. Your hosts, Jack and Jane Driscoll, describe their

Florida

guest house, built in 1937 on Lido Key, as "beach-style." The house is filled with antiques, collectibles and Ms. Driscoll's collection of shells. There is one guest room, on the ground floor, with a private bath. Guests are welcome to use the living room and laundry facilities. By prior arrangement, airport transportation will also be provided. Although guests may use the refrigerator, a continental breakfast of orange juice, fresh fruit in season, croissants with jam, bacon or ham, and coffee, tea or milk is included in the rates. Although children are welcome, there is room for only one child and one adult. The beach is one block away. Other points of interest nearby are the John Ringling Art Museum, Circum Museum and Mansion, and Jungle Gardens. It is a two-hour drive to Walt Disney World.

B & B By the Sea, 410 Garfield Dr., Lido Key, Sarasota, FL 33577; (813) 388-4039. (Write for detailed directions.) Rates are moderately expensive. Children are welcome (see above); no pets or smoking, please. Parking available at the house. Open year-round.

The Livery Stable. In 1905 when it was built, this old structure of hand-carved concrete blocks really was a livery stable. In later years the place served as a feed store, an apartment and boarding house, and a retirement home. Today the Livery Stable is a pleasant bed-and-breakfast guest house, owned by Marvin and Ingrid Jones. Its twenty rooms, ten upstairs and ten down, open onto a large central hall which once contained stalls for horses and mules. The ceilings are 9 feet, 5 inches high, and each spacious room is approximately 12

feet by 15 feet. Your hosts, who have added their own renovations to the house, offer eight rooms for guests; four of them are on the ground floor. The rooms include three singles, three doubles, one triple and one with twin beds; three baths are shared. Each guest room is furnished simply and comfortably, with easy chairs, reading lamps and cable TV. Most have desks or tables for writing. A large

Bed & Breakfast

living room at the front of the house is available for guests' use, as is the dining room. Chairs on the lower front porch and rockers on the upper porch also provide nice places to relax.

A full breakfast is included in the rates. Ingrid Jones offers guests, depending on the day, juice or fruit, eggs, pancakes, bacon or sausage, hot or cold cereal, muffins or biscuits, and coffee or tea. Other meals may be served by special arrangement. The Livery Stable is in the center of Tarpon Springs, within easy walking distance of shops, restaurants, churches and a variety of local attractions including the historic Sponge Docks area. Howard Park, with fine beaches and swimming, is nearby, and deep-sea fishing charter boats depart from the town docks.

The Livery Stable, 100 Ring Ave., Tarpon Springs, FL 33589; (813) 938-5547. (Take Alt. 19 into Tarpon Springs; the house is 3 blocks east of St. Nicholas Cathedral, at corner of Orange Street and Ring Avenue.) Rates are inexpensive, lower Nov. 1–Jan. 1, and special rates for longer stays are available. No children, please; pets are allowed only by special request. No excessive drinking or foul language, please. Street parking is available adjacent to house. Open Nov. 1–April 15.

Florida's Bed-and-Breakfast Organizations

Florida, in addition to a selection of individual guest houses, also has a growing number of bed-and-breakfast organizations. These services offer clean, comfortable, personally inspected lodgings at reasonable rates in a wide variety of private homes located all over the state. A sampling of these reservation services follows:

Bed & Breakfast of the Florida Keys, Inc., 5 Man-o-War Dr., Marathon, FL 33050; (305) 743-4118 or 743-5282. This service is owned by Joan Hopp and Naulda Bomier and includes lodgings in Marathon, Big Pine Key, Grassy Key, Duck Key, and the southeast coast of Florida.

Bed & Breakfast Co., P.O. Box 262, Miami, FL 33243; (305) 661-3270. Marcella Schaible's organization services the greater Miami area north to Melbourne and south to Key West, with other Florida areas including the Gulf, Tampa Bay, Orlando, Naples and Gainesville.

AAA Bed and Breakfast of Florida, Inc., P.O. Box 1316, Winter Park, FL 32790; (305) 628-3233. Brunhilde G. Fehner offers accommodations in central Florida, conveniently close to Disney World and other attractions, and a few along Florida's West Coast.

Florida Suncoast Bed and Breakfast, 119 Rosewood Dr., Palm Harbor, FL 33563; (813) 784-5118. Carol J. Hart's service includes private lodgings on the west coast of Florida: in the Tampa Bay area, St. Petersburg, Clearwater, Sarasota, Bradenton, and Orlando.

Georgia

Peaches and peanuts, romantic ante-bellum mansions and lofty skyscrapers, ancient Indian mounds and Civil War battlefields, islands and ocean beaches, forest-clad mountains and a vast, mysterious swamp—Georgia has them all. The largest state east of the Mississippi River, Georgia is an intriguing mixture of past and present with a diversity of scenery and a wealth of activities.

In the mid-1500s, the Spanish explorer Hernando de Soto sailed to the New World and spent most of the year 1540 roaming the territory now known as Georgia. Other Spaniards had already discovered Florida to the south, and they soon began to set up outposts there. Meanwhile, the British were busy establishing colonies northeast of Georgia, in the territory called Carolina. King George II, an ever-watchful monarch, studied the situation and spotted possible trouble ahead: Spanish forces could easily move north from Florida to invade British Carolina. Fortuitously, James Edward Oglethorpe, an English philanthropist and prison reformer, wanted to found a haven in the New World for debtors who had been released from British prisons. The king granted Oglethorpe a charter to establish a buffer colony in the region between Florida and Carolina.

In February, 1733, Oglethorpe's band of about 120 settlers (including some Europeans fleeing from religious persecution) came ashore near the site of present-day Savannah. Tomo-chi-chi, the local Cherokee chieftain, sold Oglethorpe some of his land. The colony, named Georgia in honor of the English king, coexisted more or less peacefully with the Indians for many years. Between 1738 and 1743, however, the Spanish in Florida did just what George II had feared, making several attempts to march northward. Oglethorpe stopped them each time. A man of lofty ideals and adventuresome spirit, he also proved to be a fine military leader.

When the colony's charter expired in 1752, Georgia became a royal province. Other settlers soon followed the English—Scot Highlanders, Irish, Welsh, Swiss, German and French. In the tumultuous times of the early Revolutionary War years, sympathies were fairly evenly divided between loyalty to the Crown and the desire for independence. But three Georgians signed the Declaration of Independence in 1775, and in 1788 Georgia became the fourth of the original thirteen states.

Bed & Breakfast

In the post-Revolutionary period, the state grew rapidly in population. Although its boundaries then extended all the way west to the Mississippi River, most of the region was Indian territory. The increasing need for new land to settle created confrontations, often bloody, with the Indians. In 1802 Georgia ceded all of the area west of the Chattahoochee River to the United States in return for government help in solving the Indian troubles. The Indians were banished, and their hereditary lands were divided among the newcomers.

Earlier, in the 1730s, Georgia had the unusual distinction of being the only colony to forbid slavery. The ban was short-lived for economic reasons and was repealed. Dissension concerning slavery arose again before the Civil War. The pro-slavery faction won out, and in 1861, Georgia seceded from the Union to join the Confederacy. The War devastated the state, leaving most of it in ruins. During the Reconstruction period, however, Georgia began to rise again—literally from the ashes—and embarked upon the upward push that has made it today one of the South's most prosperous and energetic states.

To make traveling easy and rewarding for the visitor, Georgia's tourist board has divided the state into scenic areas: Atlanta, the Northeast Georgia Mountains, the Classic South, the Heart of Georgia, Plains Country and the Colonial Coast. Welcome centers, operated by the state, offer information and an introductory taste of Southern hospitality.

The Atlanta Area

Everyone who has ever seen the movie *Gone With the Wind* will recall the harrowing scenes of Atlanta's fiery destruction during the Civil War. Following a 117-day siege, Union Gen. William Tecumseh Sherman's forces set a fire that destroyed all but a handful of the city's buildings. Today, Georgia's capital is the commercial center of the South—a sophisticated metropolis of skyscrapers, fine symphony and theater, art galleries, museums and parks, excellent restaurants and exciting nightlife. For shoppers, Lenox Square and nearby Phipps Plaza offer hundreds of stores including Neiman-Marcus, Lord & Taylor, Gucci, Tiffany's and the like.

Six Flags Over Georgia, a 330-acre family entertainment complex, is just beyond the city limits; Stone Mountain Park, a 3200-acre recreation area surrounding a great granite monolith, is about sixteen miles east. The late President Franklin D. Roosevelt's Little White House and Museum, in Warm Springs southeast of Atlanta, is another popular site for visitors.

The Beverly Hills Inn. Truly a find for travelers searching for an alternative to impersonal hotels or motels, the Beverly Hills Inn is

Georgia

just what it claims to be: "A charming city retreat." Located in a fine old residential area of Atlanta, the handsome structure—since 1982 a bed-and-breakfast inn—was built in 1929 and has been home to several of the city's prominent families.

Lyle Kleinhans, manager, offers guests seventeen rooms, each with a queen- or full-size bed (cots available), and five suites, each with two double beds. All of the accommodations have private baths. The rooms, with 10-foot ceilings and hardwood floors, are individually decorated with period furniture, including many antiques, and oil paintings. All include a private balcony; many have fully equipped kitchens. Five of the rooms are on the ground floor.

An elegant parlor, with a grand piano and library, is a pleasant spot for guests to gather, and there is a public swimming pool close by. A continental breakfast, included in the rates, is served in the Garden Room or outdoors on the patio in the inn's delightful small garden. The staff will help you choose one of Atlanta's fine restaurants, many within walking distance, for lunch or dinner, and will offer suggestions on things to see or do. Lenox Square is 1½ miles (five minutes) away. Also within easy reach are the Memorial Arts Center, Atlanta Historical Society, and the High Museum of Art.

The Beverly Hills Inn, 65 Sheridan Dr., N.E., Atlanta, GA 30305; (404) 233-8520. (In Buckhead, 15 minutes north of downtown Atlanta, ½ block off Peachtree Street.) Rates are expensive; weekly rates are available. Visa, American Express and MasterCard are accepted. Children are welcome; no pets, please. Parking is available. Open year-round.

Hillcrest Grove. Just half an hour north of Atlanta is neo-classic Hillcrest Grove. This turn-of-the-century country home, once known as the Hill family estate, took almost four years to build and today is nestled in a grove of pecan trees. Dennis Pitters is now your proprietor. There are three airy guest rooms available on the upper floor, all

Bed & Breakfast

with fireplaces and a welcoming bowl of fresh fruit. These guest rooms share a bath. One guest room is on the ground floor, with a fireplace and private bath. Guests are invited to use the living room, library, sitting room, formal dining room and two outside porches.

A complimentary breakfast and afternoon tea are served; baked goods are filled with pecans from the pecan grove on the grounds. A wine vinyard nearby is complete with tasting room.

Hillcrest Grove, RR 1, Box 240, Peachtree Rd., Hoschton, GA 30548; (404) 654-3425. (Two miles off I-85 and 33 miles north of Atlanta.) Rates are moderately expensive with special rates for longer stays. Children over 12 welcome; no pets, please. No smoking. Parking available at the house. Open year-round.

Georgia's Northeast Mountains
Lakemont/Mountain City/Clarkesville

This region includes a host of peaks rising more than 4000 feet. Brasstown Bald (4784 feet) is the highest. The area offers magnificent scenery: mountain views; the Chattahoochee National Forest; lovely lakes for boating, fishing and swimming, and spectacular waterfalls. Tallulah Gorge alone, 1½ miles long with a depth of 2000 feet, has three waterfalls. The movie *Deliverance* was filmed along the Chattooga, one of America's most impressive white-water rivers. If you're traveling with children, they will enjoy panning for gold at the foot of Crown Mountain, in Dahlonega's Gold Hills.

Numerous craft shops offer hand-sewn quilts, native pottery and rustic furniture. The hamlet of Helen, an old logging town, has been rebuilt to resemble a quaint Bavarian village with cobblestone streets and many attractive shops and restaurants. Helen's almost year-round calendar of festivals is highlighted by the enormously popular Octoberfest, which runs on weekends from early September to early October. The town of Clayton has a Mountaineer Festival each June, and Dillard presents a Harvest Fair in October to celebrate the region's mountain arts and crafts.

Lake Rabun Hotel. Dick and Barbara Gray graciously welcome travelers to their rustic mountain home, a two-story stone and brown-stained wood structure on the shore of Lake Rabun, right in the heart of the Chattahoochee National Forest. Indoors, the focal point of the pleasant wood-paneled lobby is a marvelous stone fireplace; in the evenings and when the air outside is nippy a cheerful, crackling fire warms chilled fingers and toes. The furniture, hand-carved of rhododendron and mountain laurel, carries out the rustic theme.

Most of the sixteen attractively furnished guest rooms have double beds. One offers three single beds, one has two double beds, and

Georgia

one includes a double bed and two cots. Six rooms have semi-private baths; one has a private half bath; the rest share a bath. Most of the rooms have sinks. (Four guest rooms are on the ground floor and have semi-private baths.) The delicious, icy, clear water is from a mountain spring, and the house is cooled throughout by fresh mountain air.

The grounds surrounding the house are wooded, with ferns, mosses and myriads of delicate wild flowers. Dogwood trees, especially lovely in the spring, shade stone paths and sturdy little stone seats provide cool places to sit. Boats may be rented at a nearby marina; a public beach is a short drive away, as are a number of the region's spectacular waterfalls.

The Grays offer guests a help-yourself, complimentary continental breakfast each morning. Guests are also invited to make use of the picnic area, grill and refrigerator. There's a good restaurant just across the road, and your hosts will be delighted to recommend others in the vicinity.

Lake Rabun Hotel, Lakemont, GA 30552; (404) 782-4946. (Nine miles south of Clayton on Lake Rabun Road. From the south, heading north from Tallulah Falls: turn left at Lakemont at the Lake Rabun sign, approximately 2 miles from Tallulah Falls, just past the campground on the right. Proceed approximately 2 miles and turn left at Lakemont Building Supplies on Lake Rabun Road; Lake Rabun Hotel is about 2 miles farther. From the north, coming south from Clayton: turn right at Wiley Junction-Convenient Store—about 6 miles—on US-441/23. Turn sharp left and proceed approximately 4 miles. Lake Rabun Hotel will be on your right.) Rates are moderate. Accommodations are limited, so early reservations are recommended. Children are welcome; no pets, please. There is parking available. Open April 1–Oct. 31.

Bed & Breakfast

York House. Beautifully situated amidst towering, century-old spruce and cedar trees, overlooking the Blue Ridge Mountains, the York House is a white, two-story inn, complete with a double-decker porch. In the early 1850s, Hiram Gibson, a plantation owner from South Carolina, bought the 1000-acre tract of land on which the York House now stands. He raised his granddaughter Mollie there and in 1873, on her fourteenth birthday, he deeded to her a 40-acre parcel on which the overseer's one-story log cabin stood. Shortly thereafter, Mollie married Civil War veteran William T. York and together they enlarged the one-story log cabin into a two-story farmhouse.

When the surveyors for the Tallulah Falls Railroad came to the area, W. T. and Mollie York took them in as guests, and the idea for an inn was born. The York family continued the tradition of innkeeping for almost 100 years until they sold the York House in 1970. Philip and Ingrid Sarris purchased the York House in 1983 and began restoring and renovating. It now has fifteen guest quarters, individually furnished with comfortable antiques, and each has its own private bathroom with natural springwater. A spacious, formal lobby and living room invite guests to relax, sit by the fireplace and swap stories about the day's adventures. A full continental breakfast is served in your room on a silver tray. The cool, tree-shaded grounds offer chairs to sit in, and there are picnic tables for outside dining across the creek by the old spring house. Several excellent restaurants are within a ten-minute drive and your host will make dinner reservations for you if you wish.

Lakes, rivers for rafting, two ski resorts, scenic mountains and hiking trails are also close by. The inn is listed in the National Register of Historic Places.

York House, P.O. Box 126, Mountain City, GA 30562; (404) 746-2068. (Located between Mountain City and Dillard, just off Rte. 441 on York House Road.)

Georgia

Rates are moderate. (Weekly and monthly rates are available upon request.) Visa and MasterCard are accepted. Well-behaved children are welcome; no pets, please. Open year-round.

The Charm House Inn. On a little knoll in the foothills of the Blue Ridge Mountains, you will find this charming Southern mansion. Built in the early 1900s by W. R. Asbury, a leading merchant in Clarkesville, the house has served as a family home, tearoom and boarding house, medical clinic, hospital, clothing outlet store and dining inn. It even went through a period of total neglect, only to be rediscovered in 1976 by your innkeeper, Ms. Mabel Fry. With such a history, it should come as no surprise that certain strange happenings have occurred which are attributed to ghosts, but Ms. Fry concludes: "We prefer to think that if indeed there are any ghosts, they are friendly and approve of us being here." How could one not approve of all the painstaking restoration that has gone on in the 5500 square feet of living space in the Greek Revival–style home?

There are six guest rooms (two on the ground floor) and all have semi-private baths and fireplaces. In addition to being welcomed with coffee, tea or soft drinks, guests enjoy a complimentary breakfast of juice, coffee or tea, milk and sausage biscuits, with applesauce and cereal.

Guests are invited to enjoy the front porch and TV parlor. Children and adults will enjoy the doll house, parlor games, and Frisbee. Or, take advantage of nearby white-water rafting, panning for gold, shopping and sightseeing, antiquing or visiting nearby Helen, Dahlonega, or the Highlands.

The Charm House Inn, US-441 (108 N. Washington), P.O. Box 392, Clarkesville, GA 30523; (404) 754-9347. Rates are moderately expensive, special rates for

Bed & Breakfast

families, longer stays, and from Sunday through Thursday nights. Children are welcome; no pets, please. MasterCard and Visa are accepted. Parking available. Open March–December.

The Classic South

Augusta

In this scenic region southeast of the mountains, travelers will find Georgia's Confederate past preserved in hundreds of magnificent ante-bellum mansions. The town of Washington has more than forty of these serene, white-columned treasures, still lived in today. Augusta, on the lovely Savannah River, also offers a fine collection of interesting buildings in its historic Olde Towne. On Telfair Street, named for Edward Telfair, Revolutionary War patriot and twice governor of Georgia, are the state's first Presbyterian Church, first medical college, Woodrow Wilson's boyhood home and the Old Government House/Courthouse Lane, built in 1801 and now headquarters for Historic Augusta, Inc.

The Telfair Inns. The Telfair Inns, located in Augusta's Olde Towne, comprise fifteen handsome Victorian mansions. Constructed between 1860 and 1890, the houses have all been beautifully restored to their former elegance. Peter S. Knox, Jr., proprietor, offers guests a choice of sixty-two double rooms and thirty-two suites. The spacious accommodations feature woodburning fireplaces, cable TV, minirefrigerators and wet bars; the suites also include kitchenettes. Thirty-five of the rooms are on the ground floor; all have private baths. Forty-four baths have whirlpools; some include bidets and fireplaces.

Georgia

The amenities offered by the inns include a lobby with fireplace and a landscaped patio and pool area with a redwood hot tub. A full Southern breakfast is included in the rates. Honeymooners and couples celebrating an anniversary are welcomed with champagne, fruit and cheese, and breakfast in bed.

The Savannah River is within walking distance, and a houseboat, the *Lady Telfair*, is available for guests. Clark Hill Reservoir nearby offers swimming, boating, fishing and water-skiing, and golfers will enjoy several fine public golf courses. The prestigious Masters Tournament is played in Augusta each April.

The Telfair Inns, 326 Greene St., Augusta, GA 30901; (404) 724-3315; in Georgia, call toll-free, (800) 282-2405; out of state (Southeast only), call (800) 241-2407. Rates are moderate to expensive, lower for longer stays. American Express, Visa, MasterCard and Carte Blanche are accepted. There is no charge for children under 13; pets under 10 pounds are allowed. Parking is available. Open year-round. Patricia P. Hardy, Manager.

The Heart of Georgia
Senoia/Macon

The region called the Heart of Georgia includes Macon, with its beautifully restored Grand Opera House; Fort Valley, where most of Georgia's famed peaches are grown, and Ocmulgee National Monument. Ocmulgee, the largest archeological Indian excavation in the East, shows the remains of Indian settlements going all the way back to 8000 B.C.

Just south of Atlanta, heading toward Columbus, is the town of Senoia. It was settled about 1830 and was named for the wife of William McIntosh (mother of William McIntosh, Jr., Chief of the Lower Creek Indians). Senoia became a town in 1860 and prospered during the time when cotton was king; it continues to flourish. Every Memorial Day weekend, Senoia hosts the McIntosh Country Fair.

The Culpepper House. Mary A. Brown operates her bed and breakfast from this turn-of-the-century home, originally built by Dr. Wilbur Culpepper, a Senoia physician for more than five decades. The exterior features gingerbread trim on the porches. Inside, stained glass, pocket sliding doors and period furniture beckon guests to revisit a bygone era. Ms. Brown has four guest rooms available, one with a private bath, none on the ground floor. The downstairs area is for guests, including the parlor, hall and den, which has a TV. The menu for the complimentary breakfast varies, but Ms. Brown often cooks zucchini or sour dough breads.

The area abounds in antiquing, craft shops and historical sites.

Bed & Breakfast

The Little White House and Callaway Gardens are approximately forty-five minutes away, and Atlanta is thirty-seven miles north.
The Culpepper House, P.O. Box 462, Senoia, GA 30276; (404) 599-8182. (Just south of Fayetteville and between Griffin and Newnan off GA-85 and GA-16.) Rates are moderate. Children over 10 are welcome; no pets, please. Your hostess asks that smoking be restricted to the downstairs. Parking available at the house. Open March 1–Dec. 31.

Hutnick House 1886. This charming Victorian house was built in 1886 by Joseph Cabaniss, an influential banker in the development of Macon, and was completely renovated in 1980. Your hosts, Fran and Ken Hutnick, offer a furnished apartment, with fully equipped kitchen, modern bath, and living room/dining area. A TV and telephone are in the apartment. Guests receive a complimentary bottle of wine and a basket of fruit, and a continental breakfast is included in the rates.

Travelers will enjoy the nearby Cannonball House, the Sidney Lanier Cottage and the Grand Opera House.

Georgia

Hutnick House 1886, 273 Orange St., Macon, GA 31201; (912) 746-5386. *(Write for brochure which includes a map.) Rates are moderately expensive, with special rates for longer stays. Visa and MasterCard are accepted. Children and pets are welcome. Off-street parking available. Open year-round.*

Plains Country

Columbus

Southwest Georgia's Plains Country includes the small town of Plains, home of Jimmy Carter, our thirty-ninth President, and the infamous Confederate military prison, Andersonville, now a national historic site with exhibits, slide shows and interpretive programs. Callaway Gardens near Pine Mountain has miles of scenic drives, walking trails and even a quail-hunting preserve. The region also contains the attractive city of Columbus, on the Chattahoochee River. The Chattahoochee Promenade, with gardens and airy gazebos, runs along the banks of the river and ties together such points of interest as the Confederate Naval Museum, Oglethorpe Monument, an open-air amphitheater and the Columbus Ironworks Convention and Trade Center. Visitors may also follow the Heritage Tour through the historic district and see the 1871 Springer Opera House (a restored Victorian theater where Edwin Booth once performed) and several historic houses. At Fort Benning, just outside the city, the National Infantry Museum offers displays tracing the evolution of the infantry from the French and Indian Wars to the present.

The DeLoffre House. History buffs will enjoy the location and background surrounding the beautifully restored DeLoffre House,

Bed & Breakfast

which dates back to 1863. The Italian-style townhouse was once owned by William L. Tillman, president of the Merchants' and Planters' Steamship Line. Tillman's niece Ethel, who later inherited the house, married Col. Samuel DeLoffre.

Paul and Shirley Romo, your present-day hosts, have five luxurious guest rooms, some with original fireplaces. There are three rooms on the ground floor. Decorated in antiques, every room has a private bath, phone, color TV and comfortable sitting area. The Romos furnish guests with a decanter of sherry and a bowl of fresh fruit, and—in case you've forgotten to pack an item or two—you will find a shaver, shampoo, shower cap and books to read! Guests are also invited to use the parlor and spacious porch, with rockers. Antiques abound throughout the house and many of the smaller items, including some lovely old clocks, are for sale.

A continental breakfast featuring homemade sweet breads and butter is included in the rates and served on antique china in the candlelit dining room each morning between 8 and 10. You'll receive a morning newspaper, too. The neighborhood's gaslit, brick-paved streets will lead you to the Promenade, Opera House and Convention Center, as well as to several fine restaurants.

The DeLoffre House, 812 Broadway, Columbus, GA 31901; (404) 324-1144. Rates are moderately expensive, with special rates for longer stays. American Express, Visa and MasterCard are accepted. Children 12 and older are welcome; no pets, please. Parking is available. Open year-round.

The Colonial Coast
Savannah/Statesboro

Georgia's Colonial Coast, about 100 miles in length, is perhaps the state's most diverse region. Here travelers will find the beguiling city of Savannah, rich in history and restored eighteenth- and early nineteenth-century houses. Offshore, a string of barrier islands runs along the Atlantic coast from Savannah south to St. Marys. Cumberland Island, with its moss-dripping live oaks, saltwater marshes, massive dunes and white-sand beaches, is accessible by passenger ferry from St. Marys. From Brunswick, one can reach Georgia's "Golden Isles," including Jekyll, Sea and St. Simons islands. The eerie Okefenokee Swamp, "land of trembling earth," lies a bit inland and extends into Florida. Once this 435,000-acre wilderness area was an ocean floor; now it is an enormous freshwater swamp where peat islands float, trembling uneasily at the tread of a foot. Cypress trees grow in broad belts, water lilies bloom in wild profusion, and alligators live there in great numbers. From entrances at Fargo, Folkston and Waycross, visitors may explore the swamp by boat. Statesboro is the home of

Georgia

Georgia Southern College and the center of diverse agricultural and manufacturing industries.

Savannah, originally laid out by Gen. James E. Oglethorpe in 1733, sits atop a bluff overlooking the Savannah River. Oglethorpe's design for the city was brilliantly conceived: a spacious, symmetrical system of houses and garden plots interspersed with handsome public squares and green parks. The plan is still imitated by modern urban designers.

In 1778, during the Revolutionary War, the British captured Savannah. A year later French and American forces tried to retake the town, but were defeated at a ghastly cost—Count Casimir Pulaski and 1700 of his men were killed during the siege. In 1782 Gen. "Mad Anthony" Wayne finally drove out the British. In the Civil War, Savannah was blockaded by the Union Navy, and General Sherman ended his march to the sea here in 1864. Rather than risk the total destruction suffered by Atlanta, the city surrendered on Dec. 22. Sherman then sent his famous message to President Lincoln: "Sir, I beg to present to you, as a Christmas gift, the city of Savannah."

The best way to appreciate Savannah's charm is to explore on foot . . . it is a strolling city. At the Visitors Center, 301 West Broad St., you can see a slide presentation and pick up descriptive material. There are also driving and bicycle routes to follow, and excellent guided bus tours. Most fun of all is to take a ride in an authentic antique carriage with your own coachman to tell you about Savannah and its history.

Although a few of the old city squares were razed in earlier, more callous times, a 2.5-square-mile area has been named a National Historic Landmark. The district encompasses some 1100 architecturally and historically important buildings, more than 1000 of which have been restored with the help of the Historic Savannah Foundation. The broad streets are lined with majestic oaks; each of the cool, serene squares has its own distinctive character, as do the many beautiful gardens and parks. Savannah's waterfront, once a rowdy hangout for sailors and pirates, now boasts a handsome promenade which, along with wrought-iron bridges and ballast-stone walkways, leads you past restored nineteenth-century cotton warehouses containing boutiques, artisans' studios, quaint pubs and restaurants.

In March more than twenty privately owned historic houses and gardens are opened to the public for tours; in April there's a walking tour of private gardens. The Savannah Arts Festival is held each May, and during the Christmas season an array of holiday observances takes place: candlelight tours of homes, Christmas concerts, carolers, and even a traditional British Yule Feast.

Not least among Savannah's attractions are her many exceptionally inviting guest houses. Most are in the historic district and have lengthy histories, distinguished architecture, working fireplaces and secluded, brick-walled courtyards. Choosing which house to try may

Bed & Breakfast

be the most difficult decision you'll make during your stay. Of course, you could plan to remain indefinitely and experience them all. As one proud citizen says: "Savannah is so interesting and beautiful, there's no need to go elsewhere!"

Statesboro Inn. Owners Bill and Bonnie Frondorf extend an offer to hang your hat on their hall tree and relax. Their business, they say, is to take care of you! The Statesboro Inn was built in 1904, but it wasn't until 1985 that it was completely restored to include central heat and air conditioning, remote control TV and modern baths. Nine guestrooms await weary travelers. Three rooms are on the ground floor, and all nine have private baths. Some rooms have fireplaces and two rooms have whirlpool tubs. All are decorated in antiques, each room of a different period or design. A turn-down bed service and bedtime treat, as well as a complimentary continental breakfast and newspaper, are touches that make the Statesboro Inn so special.

Guests are invited to use the parlor for reading and games and the dining room for breakfast and special events; the front and rear porches, brick patio and shady grounds are for enjoyment. A restored cabin on the grounds serves as a quaint gift shop filled with antiques and country collectibles.

Statesboro is conveniently located just fifty minutes from Savannah, two hours from Macon, and just a short drive from South Carolina or the Florida border.

Statesboro Inn, 106 S. Main St., Statesboro, GA 30458; (912) 489-8628. (The Inn is located on US-301, just a few blocks off US-80, in downtown Statesboro.) Rates range from moderately expensive to expensive, with special rates for longer stays. American Express, Visa and MasterCard are accepted. Children are welcome; no pets, please. There is ample parking at the Inn. Open year-round.

Georgia

Morel House. Built in the 1800s, this charming, four-story wooden frame house overlooks Orleans Square and is in the heart of the historic district. Ms. Mary Ann Smith offers two guest rooms (actually a garden-level apartment). There are a full and a half bath, a large living room with a working fireplace, and a kitchen with eating area. A complimentary continental breakfast of tea, coffee, juice and homemade Danish is provided.

Guests are within walking distance of River Street, churches, shops, museums and the Civic Center.

Morel House, 117 W. Perry St., Savannah, GA 31401; (912) 234-4088. Rates are moderately expensive with discounts for off-season and longer stays. Children are welcome; no pets, please. Parking available. Open year-round.

"417," The Haslam-Fort House. Alan Fort, your convivial host, is a converted Savannahian who says he is in love with his adopted city and its treasures. "Most Savannahians," he notes, "are walking Chamber of Commerce addicts in their own right, and I seem to fall into the same category. Forgive me, but it's infectious!" His home in the historic district is within a ten-minute walk of most of the city's other historic highlights. A three-story brick townhouse in the Italianate style, it is unusual in that it does not have a high stoop entrance to the parlor floor and does include a full side yard, now a garden.

The place was built in 1872 for John Haslam, an independent entrepreneur who produced minstrel shows after the Civil War. Haslam was lynched in a town in Ohio when he angered an eager audience by failing to put on the show. His ghost (so says Mr. Fort) still resides on the third floor of the Savannah house (once a Savannahian, always a Savannahian) and can occasionally be heard

Bed & Breakfast

stomping around in the late evenings. He and Mr. Fort are, you'll be glad to hear, quite friendly due to their mutual affection for the house.

Guests will find a delightful garden suite with two bedrooms, a spacious living room with fireplace, full kitchen and bath, telephone, radio and TV. The high-ceilinged, airy rooms are furnished with antiques mixed with comfortable miscellany. The accommodations are suitable for a couple, a family or two couples traveling together. Cribs and baby sitters are provided if requested. The suite, centrally air conditioned and heated, is entirely separate from the rest of the house and comprises the entire garden floor. Entry is to the west of the house through the garden, which guests are encouraged to use.

Coffee, tea, Sanka (and a coffee maker), orange juice, English muffins, bagels and fresh pastry are provided on a self-serve basis, included in the rates. The suite's refrigerator is stocked with soft drinks, and if you like, Mr. Fort will suggest a caterer for dinners. Your host, a former actor and New York advertising account executive, speaks German, Norwegian, Spanish and some French. He acts as a concierge for his guests, arranging reservations for dinner, theater and tours, and is eager to help guests enjoy Savannah in every possible way. He's also a real estate agent and will sell you a house if you decide to stay on permanently!

"417," The Haslam-Fort House, 417 E. Charlton St., Savannah, GA 31401; (912) 233-6380. (Between Habersham and Price streets, adjacent to Troup Square.) Rates are expensive, lower for longer stays. Children are welcome. Pets are welcome (limit 2 with a one-time charge of $10 each). Free parking is available in the lane directly behind the house. Open year-round.

The Ballastone Inn. If you've ever cherished a dream of being utterly pampered, a stay at Savannah's Ballastone Inn will fulfill virtually your every wish. Operated on the lines of an elegant, small European hostelry, the Ballastone offers an array of comforting amenities ranging from a welcoming glass of port or sherry to white Dior terry cloth robes in the bath. Shoes left outside your door will be polished overnight; breakfast—served in your room or in the courtyard—starts off the morning in gracious Southern style; late afternoon tea is provided as a relaxing break in the day's activities. And when you're ready to head for bed, you'll find a praline on the pillow.

Opened as a bed-and-breakfast inn in 1981, the Ballastone is named for the old stones brought from Europe as ballast by the ships calling at Savannah's busy port. These stones were used as paving on River Street and adjoining ramps. Tarby and Leslie Bryant purchased the place, built in 1835 as a private home, in the late 1970s. Tarby, with a group of partners, entered the hotel field as an investment. (The group also manages the Telfair Inns in Augusta.) His wife, Leslie, has a master's degree in art history; while Tarby handled the restoration of the house, she was responsible for the furnishings and interior

Georgia

decorations. Paula Palmer and Larry Wilkes act as resident hosts and concierges.

There are nineteen rooms and suites for guests, each appointed with its own unique Victorian character. Typical Savannah colors and patterns have been used throughout, including fabrics from the Historic Savannah Collection of Scalamandre silks. Authentic eighteenth- and nineteenth-century antiques include marble-topped tables and dressers, cheval mirrors, armoires, love seats and wing chairs. The beds, mostly rice posters in queen- or king-size, are new but faithful reproductions, for guests' comfort, and the baths have all been modernized. Fifteen of the rooms feature fireplaces; all have private baths and air conditioning, and all except those on the garden level have ceiling fans as well. Five of the rooms are on the ground floor.

The cozy downstairs parlor, with a fireplace and fabric-covered walls, is furnished with an eclectic assortment of antiques, including a Victorian piano and horsehair sofa. From the parlor balcony you

Bed & Breakfast

look down upon a terraced garden courtyard with jasmine, gardenias, greenery and a tinkling fountain.

Breakfast, included in the rates, offers freshly squeezed fruit juice, perhaps a slice of melon, just-baked hot muffins, pots of jam and marmalade, and excellent coffee or tea. The repast is served on pretty china and accompanied by a morning newspaper. In the afternoon, guests are invited to take tea along with Southern-style sweets and cocktail nibbles. If you'd like to take some of the latter home, Cookie Byrd's Benne Bits (a Savannah specialty), pralines and peach-leather candy are available for purchase; you will find them in a large secretary, which acts as a "gift shop," in the entrance hall.

The Ballastone Inn, 14 E. Oglethorpe Ave., Savannah, GA 31401; (912) 236-1484. Rates are expensive, free for children under 12. American Express, Visa and MasterCard are accepted. Children are welcome; small pets are allowed, with a nonrefundable $15 fee. Limited off-street parking and ample meter parking (no charge for out-of-state licenses) are available. Open year-round.

The Liberty Inn 1834. Frank and Janie Harris may well be the busiest couple in the South, let alone in Savannah. Not only do they own the Liberty Inn—they also operate three Savannah restaurants: the Regency, the Shrimp Factory and the River House!

The Harrises' inn, a three-story, clapboard-over-brick, Federal-style structure, was built in 1834 by Col. William Thorne Williams of the Chatham Legion of Militia. Williams, who was also a publisher and bookseller, served six terms as mayor of Savannah. During the late 1800s, under different ownership, the house was one of Savannah's most popular gathering places. In the 1930s the building was turned into a rooming house and cafe; by the 1970s, however, it had been abandoned.

The Harrises, who had visited the cafe back in 1949 on their first date, had a sentimental attachment to the place. They purchased it in 1968 and, in 1978, began the difficult work of restoration, carefully preserving the original brick fireplaces, exposed beams and interior brick walls. Thirteen months later, they reopened the once-again stately townhouse, with five spacious suites for guests. Each suite is painted in Historic Savannah Tabby White, one of the colors commonly used during the city's Colonial era. The rooms, all different, are furnished with comfortable beds, period pieces and antiques. Paintings and silk flowers add to their appeal, and the Harrises have placed books on Savannah's history in each room for visitors' enjoyment.

Three of the suites are on the lower level of the house. All have individually controlled air conditioning, private phone and color cable TV, and all but one feature fireplaces. There are three two-bedroom suites and two with one bedroom; all have extra sofa beds, a family/sitting room, fully equipped kitchen, modern bath, ample closet space, wall-to-wall carpeting and a laundry center with washer and dryer. Each suite has its own private entrance to the large courtyard, which has an 8-foot "Super Spa" and gas-fired grill. And, a complimentary decanter of peach schnapps is provided. In the fall, guests may pick grapes in the landscaped courtyard; the cypress fence supports six different varieties.

Breakfast fixings (orange juice, Danish and coffee) are provided in every suite, included in the rates. For other meals, you are cordially invited to try one of the Harrises' restaurants, or they will recommend others. Your hosts, by the way, are a mine of information about Georgia's history and legends. Ask them to tell the story behind Chatham Artillery Punch, Savannah's most noted drink—a bracing concoction of Catawba wine, rum, gin, brandy, Benedictine, whiskey, strong tea, brown sugar, orange and lemon juice, and cherries. And that's only the base. Champagne is added just before serving! If you've the courage to try it, the brew is served at the Shrimp Factory and River House.

The Liberty Inn 1834, 128 W. Liberty St., Savannah, GA 31401; (912) 233-1007. Rates are expensive and vary according to the suite; group rates are available, and there is a 15% discount for monthly stays, 10% for 7 or more days. American Express, Visa and MasterCard are accepted. Children with parents are welcome; no pets, please. Private and on-street parking are available. Open year-round.

The Eliza Thompson House. A "carriage house inn," the Eliza

Bed & Breakfast

Thompson House was built in 1847. This beautifully restored townhouse in Savannah's historic district was originally the home of Eliza Shaffer Thompson, intriguingly described as a "ravishing redhaired widow" and renowned for her gracious hospitality. Its equally hospitable present-day hosts have preserved many of the house's finest features, including gleaming heart-pine floors and numerous fireplaces.

The twenty-five elegantly appointed guest rooms (six on the ground floor) reflect a bygone era. Each not only has a private bath, color TV and climate control, but also is furnished with antique reproductions and authentic pieces. A lavish continental breakfast, included in the rates, consists of juice, freshly baked butter croissants, fruit conserve marmalade, homemade Benedict cheesecake, plus tea and freshly ground coffee. On arrival, guests are welcomed with a glass of sherry or champagne, and a bottle of imported wine waits in each guest room.

The Eliza Thompson House, 5 W. Jones St., Savannah, GA 31401; (800)

Georgia

348-9378 or (800) 447-4667 from in-state. (At the corner of Jones and Bull streets.) Rates are expensive; package plans are available. Visa, MasterCard and American Express are accepted. Children are welcome (under 5, no charge; 6-18, $5 extra; 18 and older, $10 extra); no pets, please. Private parking is available. Open year-round.

Bed and Breakfast Inn. An 1853 Federalist home built as the Savannah residence of a wealthy cotton plantation owner, this handsome townhouse was constructed of bricks handmade by slaves. Bob McAlister, your host, has four ground-level suites for guests: each offers a bedroom, fully equipped kitchen, sitting room, bath, private phone, television and a separate entrance. In addition, there are several nicely decorated upstairs bedrooms, which share a bath. Mr. McAlister owns a fine collection of primitive art from Mexico, New Guinea and the Middle East, displayed in the house's living room, which boasts a 14-foot ceiling and barn siding paneling. Other interesting features include beautifully restored ironwork, a number of secret hiding places, and—according to your host—a resident, harmless ghost. There's a courtyard, too, with a lovely garden and fountain. Breakfast, included in the rates, consists of orange juice, special Savannah pastries, grits, eggs, cold cereal and coffee.
Bed and Breakfast Inn, 117 W. Gordon St., Savannah, GA 31401; (912) 238-0518. (At Chatham Square.) Rates are moderate to expensive. American Express, Visa and MasterCard are accepted. Well-behaved children are welcome; no pets, please. On-street parking is available. Open year-round.

The Oglethorpe Inn. In the heart of Savannah's historic district is the mid-nineteenth-century Oglethorpe Inn. Ms. Doris B. Pierce, your hostess, takes great pride in providing the charm of old Savannah along with the modern conveniences: gas log fireplaces, ceiling fans

Bed & Breakfast

in each room, private telephones and color TVs. The inn is furnished with period pieces and some antiques. Handmade pillows decorate the beds and a conversation-piece "old church pew." An antique switchboard is in the front lobby and still serves as part of the phone system! There are five guest rooms available (one on the ground floor), and all have private baths and living areas. A complimentary, continental breakfast consists of juice, pastry or biscuits, coffee, tea or milk. At night, the turn-down service leaves a mint by the bed. Guests are within easy walking distance of restaurants, shopping and all of Savannah's historical sites.

The Oglethorpe Inn, 117 W. Oglethorpe Ave., P.O. Box 9803, Savannah, GA 31412; (912) 232-2700. Rates range from moderate to expensive, lower for longer stays. American Express, Visa and MasterCard are accepted. Children are welcome; no pets, please. Parking available. Open year-round.

Charlton Court. Charlton Court, facing Troup Square, is of Greek Revival architecture, built in 1851. The house was the childhood home of actor Charles Coburn and now belongs to Jerry and Isabella Reeves. Guest accommodations are in the former carriage house, overlooking the courtyard. Included are a spacious living room and bedroom with heart pine floors, high ceilings and fireplaces, a fully equipped kitchen and a modern bath. Visitors enter the guest quarters through a private garden walkway, then up a wrought-iron staircase. The rooms, furnished in traditional style with antiques, contain part of Mrs. Reeves' doll collection. The bedroom has a double bed; the sofa in the living room opens up into a double bed, and there is a crib if needed. Continental breakfast and a welcoming bottle of wine are included in the rates. Your hosts will be pleased to provide information about museums, tours and restaurants, and there are two bicycles for guests' use.

Charlton Court, 403 E. Charlton St., Savannah, GA 31401; (912) 236-2895. (On Troup Square in the historic district.) Rates are expensive, lower for stays of 1 week or longer; there is no charge for children under 12. No pets, please. Parking is available. Open year-round.

Louisiana

> Beautiful is the land, with its prairies
> and forests of fruit-trees;
> Under the feet a garden of flowers,
> and the bluest of heavens
> Bending above, and resting its dome
> on the walls of the forest.
> They who dwell there have named it
> the Eden of Louisiana.

These lines by Henry Wadsworth Longfellow may not be as familiar as "This is the forest primeval ... the murmuring pines and the hemlocks," but they are also part of his narrative poem *Evangeline*. For many travelers, Louisiana means "Evangeline Country," that region of the state where Acadian exiles settled after being driven from their Canadian homes in the eighteenth century. Although Longfellow created his own romantic version of the tragic exodus, the basic tale is a true one.

Acadia, now Nova Scotia and New Brunswick, was first settled by French colonists. It later became a British possession; in 1755, the British ordered the Acadians to renounce their Roman Catholic faith and swear allegiance to the Crown. They refused, so were dispossessed of their land and dispersed to various sites including New England, France and the Indies. Some of them made their way to Louisiana, originally a French colony settled in the 1600s. Although the region was under Spanish rule at the time, the authorities welcomed the new arrivals and gave them grants of land.

That new world must have seemed incredibly exotic and strange to those weary emigrants from far-off Canada. In Louisiana the Acadians found a semi-tropical region of great rivers and sleepy bayous, marshes, mysterious cypress swamps and rich soil. Different though it was, the hardworking, deeply religious newcomers adapted quickly to their new surroundings and soon became valued members of the colony. In later years, many more Acadians came to Louisiana; their descendants, some of whom still speak an intriguing mixture of French and English, live there today. They are called Cajuns, a form of the word Acadian.

Seven governments have ruled Louisiana over the years: French, Spanish, English, the Republic of West Florida, the Republic of Louisiana, the Confederate States of America and the United States. The tangled tale began in the 1500s with the Spanish adventurer Hernando

Bed & Breakfast

de Soto. De Soto was searching for a golden empire similar to the Incas'; what he actually discovered—in 1541—was the Mississippi River. A century later, Robert Cavelier, Sieur de La Salle, voyaged down the Mississippi and claimed the region for France, naming it Louisiana for the French monarch Louis XIV. The first permanent settlement was established in 1714 at Natchitoches; New Orleans was founded four years later.

In 1763, France ceded Louisiana west of the Mississippi, plus New Orleans, to Spain, and the region east of the river (except for New Orleans) to England. The British ruled their section, called the Florida Parishes, until 1781, when it became part of Spanish Louisiana. The Acadians, who settled there during that period, were joined by French aristocrats fleeing the Revolution in France and by wealthy plantation owners escaping slave uprisings in the West Indies. In 1800 Spain ceded all of Louisiana except the Florida Parishes back to France. Then in 1803 President Thomas Jefferson bought the vast Louisiana Territory from Napoleon Bonaparte for $15 million, clinching one of the biggest real estate deals in our history. The almost one million square miles of new land which comprised the Louisiana Purchase later became part or all of the states of Louisiana, Missouri, Arkansas, Iowa, Minnesota, North Dakota, South Dakota, Nebraska, Kansas, Oklahoma, Wyoming, Montana and Colorado.

The Florida Parishes, however, were still owned by Spain. In 1810, a band of American settlers there staged a rebellion, captured Baton Rouge, and established the independent West Florida Republic. In 1812, Louisiana became a state and was admitted to the Union. In 1861, at the start of the Civil War, Louisiana seceded to become an independent republic, a condition which lasted only fifty-five days. Louisiana then joined the Confederacy and, after the war ended, was readmitted to the Union in 1868.

Louisiana's French and Spanish heritage is still very evident. The French Napoleonic Code, rather than Common Law, is the basis of law in the state. New Orleans, in particular, reflects eighteenth-century Spanish Colonial rule with its lacy, wrought-iron architecture, and counties in Louisiana are still called parishes, a custom that goes back to the Spanish era. Other contributions to the state's ethnic melting pot have been made by English and German settlers, and later by Italians, Irish, Yugoslavians and Hungarians. And blacks: slaves transported from Africa brought along many of their own traditions, including the beginnings of jazz.

North Louisiana

Ruston

North Louisiana is typically Deep South, with many ante-bellum

Louisiana

homes and several Civil War battlefields. It is a peaceful, rural region, through which runs the Red River. An enormous log jam called "the great raft" once blocked the river for about 180 miles. In 1835 a riverboat captain named Henry Miller Shreve (later the founder of Shreveport) invented an ingenious "snagboat." Using his invention as a battering ram, he formed a channel through the woody debris, opening the river upstream from Natchitoches for navigation.

Shreveport today is the home of the Louisiana State Fair, held each October, and also of the famous country music show "Louisiana Hayride" (Elvis Presley got his start there). Flower lovers will enjoy the American Rose Society Gardens nearby, a 118-acre expanse of roses and camellias. There is Fort Humbug, too, where Confederate forces tricked enemy scouts by placing charred logs to look like cannons. Natchitoches (pronounced Nak-e-tash), the oldest settlement in the Louisiana Purchase territory, lies southeast of Shreveport. Roque House Museum, a rustic, 1803 plantation building, offers a fine example of a French Colonial house with mud, moss and cypress-beam construction. For an entertaining lesson in local history, try to see *Louisiana Cavalier*, a lively outdoor musical drama. It tells the story of French explorer Louis Juchereau de St. Denis, who founded Natchitoches in 1714, and depicts his struggles to establish friendly relations with the Indians and Spanish. The play is presented on weekend evenings between June and late August.

Just east of Shreveport, off I-20, is the quaint town of Ruston. State parks and lakes are within fifteen miles; there are golf courses, and the Passion Play is done in Calhoun, approximately five miles away.

Twin Gables. Built in rural Lincoln Parish by the Knowles family in 1882, this charming bed and breakfast was moved piece by piece to Ruston in 1890 after the arrival of the railroad. Today, it rests in the heart of the town. Carol Hudson and Beulah Laster have made five charming guest rooms available. All the rooms are on the ground floor with private baths. Connecting rooms are also available to accommodate family groups or two couples traveling together.

Guests are invited to enjoy breakfast either in the dining room or on a tray in the garden, on the front porch or in the privacy of their own rooms. The complimentary continental fare consists of gourmet coffees and sweet rolls. Also available for guests is a TV in the dining room and a comfortable living room where magazines and books are available.

Twin Gables, 711 N. Vienna, Ruston, LA 71270; (318) 255-4452, 255-8677 or 255-8026. Rates are moderately expensive, with special rates for longer stays. Visa and MasterCard are accepted. Children are welcome; no pets, please. Sorry, no smoking allowed. Parking available at the house. Open year-round.

Bed & Breakfast

Acadiana

Acadiana is "Evangeline Country," composed of twenty-two parishes forming an enormous triangle in southwest Louisiana. Here you'll find the unique Cajun culture still surviving in the language, the music and the cuisine. Fishing and fur trapping are still major occupations along the region's rivers and bayous; Louisiana leads the country in fur production. The town of Lafayette is considered the unofficial capital of Acadiana. Visit the Acadian Village and Tropical Gardens, five miles south, to see what an early Cajun bayou village looked like. Included are a number of restored buildings and splendid gardens.

Longfellow's poem *Evangeline* was based (very loosely) on a real-life romance between two young Acadians—Emmeline Labiche (Evangeline) and Louis Arceneaux (Gabriel). In historic St. Martinville, not far from Lafayette, the Evangeline Monument marks the grave of Emmeline Labiche. St. Martinville was settled by Acadians in the late 1700s; during the French Revolution Royalist refugees from France arrived and turned the village into a miniature version of Paris with grand balls, operas and other elegant events. The Petit Paris Museum contains a fine collection of furniture, Mardi Gras costumes and other artifacts once owned by the aristocratic French settlers. At the Longfellow-Evangeline Commemorative Area near town, visitors can explore the Acadian House Museum. Supposedly, the eighteenth-century building once belonged to Louis Arceneaux, Evangeline's beloved Gabriel.

Baton Rouge/St. Francisville/New Iberia

East of Acadiana, on the other side of the Mississippi, is Baton Rouge, Louisiana's capital. Be sure to see the impressive Capitol Building; from its observation tower there's a marvelous view of the city and surrounding countryside. Other interesting sites to visit are the Old State Capitol, the old and the present governors' mansions, the Louisiana State University campus and the Greater Baton Rouge Zoo. The name Baton Rouge, by the way, means "red stick." Long ago, according to the records of early French explorers, a post—probably a red cypress—marked the boundary between the lands of two Indian tribes.

Louisiana has some sixty plantation mansions and ante-bellum homes that are open to the public, scattered throughout the state. The area surrounding St. Francisville, about twenty-five miles north of Baton Rouge, offers an array of these beautiful structures. Rosedown Plantation, a handsomely restored example of ante-bellum opulence, is located half a mile east of town on routes 61 and 10. In addition to a magnificent oak alley (avenue), there are twenty-eight acres of gardens with flowers, greenery, ornamental statuary and charming gazebos. The mansion, built in 1835, contains a wealth of paintings, murals and antique furnishings. The Myrtles, one mile north on Route

Louisiana

61, is of French-style architecture. Constructed in 1795, it features a 110-foot-long gallery.

Catalpa, 4½ miles north on Route 6, is a reconstruction of the original plantation house which burned shortly after the Civil War. A pleasant, late-Victorian home filled with family treasures of five generations, Catalpa is situated in a parklike setting of thirty acres of gardens. Oakley Plantation, four miles south of St. Francisville on Route 61 and then left on Route 965, includes a 100-acre Audubon Wildlife Sanctuary. John James Audubon once stayed in the West Indies–style house while painting some of his famous *Birds of America*. Rosemont, Jefferson Davis's boyhood home, is farther out, about twenty-five miles north of St. Francisville. Ask at the West Feliciana Historical Society Museum in St. Francisville for information on all of these and many other homes in the area. Some of the plantation houses are open year-round, others only in season or by appointment.

If you're heading for New Orleans next, you will find yet another of Louisiana's famous plantations on the way. Follow Route 10 northeast to Route 22 and across Sunshine Bridge to Route 18. The plantation, Oak Alley, is situated between St. James and Vacherie. In the early 1700s a French settler, whose name is not known, built a small house on the site of the present mansion. He planted twenty-eight live oaks in two well-spaced rows reaching from his house to the Mississippi. (The river, however, cannot now be seen from the property or even from the road; it runs behind a grass-covered levee.)

In any case, the quarter-mile alley of oaks is now more than 250 years old. The magnificent Greek Revival mansion that stands at its end was built between 1837 and 1839 by Jacques Telesphore Roman, a wealthy French sugar planter, for his new bride. But by the early years of this century, the house had fallen into disrepair. Andrew and Josephine Stewart purchased the place in 1925, and Oak Alley became the first of the Great River Road plantations to be renovated. Considered one of the finest examples of adaptive restoration in the region, the mansion may be toured year-round except on Thanksgiving, Christmas and New Year's Day.

Mount Hope Plantation Home and Gardens. Owners Mr. and Mrs. Jack Dease welcome guests to Mount Hope Plantation with, appropriately, mint juleps! One of the oldest homes in Baton Rouge, the house was built in 1817 by Joseph Sharp, a German planter. Sharp, who had come to Louisiana in 1786, settled on a 400-acre Spanish land grant. His home, a typical planter's house of the era, included high ceilings, spacious rooms, white wooden mantels, solid cypress entry doors, and a lengthy veranda along the front. During the Civil War, or War Between the States as Southerners prefer to call it, Mount Hope Plantation served as an encampment to provide rest for weary Confederate troops and their horses.

The Deases have carefully restored the old house, which is listed

Bed & Breakfast

in the National Register of Historic Sites, and furnished it with exquisite antiques. Three guestrooms are available on the ground floor, one of which is a two-bedroom suite with bath. The other guest room also has a private bath. Guests are welcome to enjoy the house's lovely parlor with wood-burning fireplace and period furnishings, and the veranda. The grounds, featuring broad lawns and century-old live oaks, include a charming boxwood garden with an iron fountain cast in Boston in 1830. There's also a gift shop on the property.

Included in the rates is a hearty Plantation Breakfast of fresh fruit, homemade biscuits, grits, eggs, ham or bacon and French-drip coffee with chicory, served in the dining room by a butler. (Other meals may be arranged by appointment.) Restaurants and shops are nearby, but you'll need a car. Mount Hope and its gardens are open to the public for tours from 9 to 5 daily.

Mount Hope Plantation, 8151 Highland Rd., Baton Rouge, LA 70808; (504) 766-8600. (Five minutes from Baton Rouge.) Rates are moderately expensive. No children, please, and no pets. Parking is available. Open year-round except Christmas Day.

The Cottage Plantation. One of the few complete ante-bellum plantations remaining in the South, the Cottage—which is open to the public for tours—is on Route 61, five miles north of St. Francisville. Leaving the main road, you follow a long, winding drive through the woods, ending—surprisingly—in a vista of hills and meadows that looks amazingly like Vermont. On the grounds are the main house,

Louisiana

with accommodations for guests, and a large collection of outbuildings, including the old schoolhouse, kitchen, milk house, carriage house, barn, slave quarters, commissary and smoke house.

At first glance the rambling, two-story main house looks rather like an English farm cottage, but with an exceptionally long front gallery. Actually it is a series of buildings joined together, erected between 1795 and 1859. The earliest part of the house was designed in the Spanish tradition with square, airy chambers, each opening onto a gallery through tall door-windows. The transoms also exhibit the Spanish influence, with their delicate, curving fretwork. The tall blinds have stationary slats; these were installed to thwart the local Indians' inquisitive nighttime habit of prowling around outdoors and peering in at the inhabitants!

The last section of the house to be built was the 65-foot-long great wing; its front gallery adjoins the back gallery of the original building. Except for the massive poplar sills, the Cottage was constructed entirely of virgin cypress. All of the woodwork, including the galleries' pillars, is hand-wrought.

The plantation was originally a Spanish land grant acquired by John Allen and Patrick Holland. Thomas Butler purchased the place around 1811. Butler, a native of Pennsylvania, moved first to the Mississippi Territory, then to Louisiana where he later served as a state congressman and judge for many years. He died in 1847 and is buried in a small, walled cemetery on the grounds. A number of famous people have been guests at the Cottage, including Andrew Jackson, who stayed here en route to Natchez shortly after the Battle of New Orleans.

Mr. and Mrs. J. Edward Brown are the present-day owners; Mr. and Mrs. Robert H. Weller act as managers. Five double rooms and one single are available for guests, some with double beds, some with twin beds. All have private baths and are air conditioned. Three of the rooms are on the ground floor. The house is furnished throughout with antiques, many dating back to the Civil War era or earlier. The rates include coffee delivered to your room each morning, breakfast served in the elegant dining room, and a tour of the entire house, outbuildings and grounds. The lavish breakfast consists of juice, eggs, bacon, grits, biscuits and coffee.

Outdoors, from the south galleries, guests look out at the old plantation buildings. The north gallery overlooks a woodland of ancient live oaks, magnolias, poplars, beeches, hollies, crape myrtle, dogwood and evergreens. Fenced English gardens at the ends of the long galleries boast superb azaleas and japonicas—over a century old, and as tall as large trees. Beyond are green pastures; the tiny old cemetery lies at the edge of one of them. An outdoor swimming pool is a contemporary addition to the grounds, and the old plantation kitchen now houses an antique and gift shop.

The Cottage Plantation, Rte. 5, Box 425, St. Francisville, LA 70775; (504) 635-3674. (At Cottage Lane.) Rates are moderate to expensive. Children are

Bed & Breakfast

welcome; no pets, please. Parking is available. Open year-round, except Christmas.

Mintmere Plantation House. "Guests" were not always welcome at Mintmere. During the Civil War, a skirmish was fought on the property, and later, when the town of New Iberia was occupied by Union troops in 1863, the house became the "uninvited" headquarters of Gen. Alfred Lee, the famous "Kansas-judge-turned-warrior." Since that time, the years brought deterioration and the house was actually slated for demolition until Dr. Roy Boucvalt purchased it in 1976. Today, this Greek Revival raised cottage overlooks the historic Bayou Teche. It has been completely restored to its former elegance, furnished with Louisiana-made antique pieces made between 1790 and 1880. Five guest rooms are available, three in Mintmere and two in the West Indies Cottage. Two bedrooms in Mintmere share a sitting room and bath; this suite is rented only to a family of four people who are traveling together. For children under the age of 11, the accommodations are in the West Indies Cottage with a rollaway bed provided at no extra cost. Rooms are actually suites which include a bedroom, private sitting room and bath. Two guest bedrooms are on the "ground" floor, but since this house is a raised cottage, the ground floor is approximately 8 feet off the ground. People who are incapacitated in any way may find the steps difficult to maneuver.

The first leader of the exiled Acadians to arrive in Teche country was Joseph "Beausoleil" Broussard. The Armand Broussard House, circa 1790, is located on the Mintmere grounds and was named for Joseph Broussard's son, born in Acadia in 1754. The Broussard House is the oldest house in Iberia Parish and was moved to Bayou Teche. The "bousillage" construction (comprised of mud and moss) house has the original floors, doors, mantels and hand-wrought iron hardware. The West Indies Cottage, circa 1815, used for guest rooms, was moved to its present location and restored by Dr. Boucvalt.

Louisiana

Visitors to Mintmere are within easy walking distance to the New Iberia Historical District and about one mile from Shadows-on-the-Teche. Included in the rates is a tour of Mintmere and the Armand Broussard House. Guests are also free to use the Mintmere parlor. A full, complimentary breakfast is served each morning in the dining room. Jane Breaux, the manager, will assist guests in reservations and information regarding the area. Persons who are not guests of Mintmere may take guided tours daily between 10 a.m. and 4 p.m., except for the holidays listed below.

Mintmere Plantation House, 1400 E. Main St., New Iberia, LA 70560; (318) 364-6210. Rates are expensive. Children are welcome (see limitations above); no pets, please. Parking is available at the house. Closed Thanksgiving, Christmas Eve/Day, New Year's Eve/Day and Easter Eve/Day.

New Orleans

New Orleans is an old city within a new one, a large city that is full of *little* places. Despite its size, it has an air of intimacy: it is a city of neighborhoods, narrow streets and byways, of gardens and hidden courtyards. One of America's most picturesque and cosmopolitan cities, New Orleans has an ambiance distinctly its own.

Jean Baptiste Lemoyne, Sieur de Bienville, founded New Orleans in 1718. Lemoyne, governor of the Louisiana colony, named the settlement for the Duc d'Orleans, then regent of France. In 1763, when France ceded Louisiana to Spain and England, New Orleans became a Spanish possession. The town's French citizens were not at all happy over that turn of events and for a brief period tried to overthrow Spanish rule. Then, in 1800, New Orleans was ceded back to France; twenty days later, to the shocked chagrin of the inhabitants, France sold the city, along with the rest of the Louisiana Territory, to the United States.

During the next few years Americans came to New Orleans in large numbers, doubling the population and bringing in much-needed money. In 1812, the city became Louisiana's capital (the capital was shifted about after 1849 and finally settled in Baton Rouge in 1882). The British attacked New Orleans in 1815, near the end of the War of 1812, but were defeated by Gen. Andrew Jackson. Half a century later, in 1862, the Union fleet captured the city and held it until the end of the Civil War. After the difficult Reconstruction years, New Orleans once again began to prosper and today is one of the country's busiest international ports.

Most visitors start out with a walking or horse-drawn carriage tour of the French Quarter, or Vieux Carre, meaning "Old Square." More Spanish than French in appearance, the French Quarter, laid out in a gridiron plan in 1721, is bounded by Iberville, Esplanade and North Rampart streets and the Mississippi River. Much of the original city was destroyed by fire in the late 1700s, and the Spanish rulers of that day rebuilt in their own style, creating the arches, balconies and courtyards that are still so typical of the Quarter. On Royal Street you'll find a profusion of antique shops; facing Jackson Square, the heart of the old city, are three handsome eighteenth-century structures: the Cabildo, the St. Louis Cathedral and the Presbytere. Dotted throughout the Quarter are dozens of historic houses, many open to the public.

Some waterfront cities, such as San Francisco and Boston, are built on hills and have sweeping views of the water. But flat New Orleans lies 10 feet below the level of the Gulf of Mexico, and 3 to 6 feet below the Mississippi River's high-water level. So the city is surrounded by earthen levees to protect it from flooding, and the river is pretty much invisible except from the levees. On the far side of Jackson Square, a lengthy section of levee is also a promenade. Named the Moon Walk after former Mayor "Moon" Landrieu, the walkway offers flowers, fountains and benches, and it is a grand place to watch the busy river traffic.

The other area of New Orleans most beloved by visitors is the Garden District, which begins on the far side of Canal Street. Settled by Americans who arrived after the Louisiana Purchase transaction, the residential Garden District is easily reached by bus or the St. Charles streetcar. Take the latter; you'll love it. The trolley clangs its leisurely way for 6½ miles from downtown out through the Garden District and on to Carrolton. The route passes elegant old Greek Revival mansions, lovely gardens and green squares galore, handsome churches, parts of Tulane and Loyola universities, and the superb Audubon Zoo. Incidentally, New Orleans' streetcar system is excellent and costs very little to use, even with unlimited stops.

New Orleans is the birthplace of jazz. For a memorable experience, pay a visit to Preservation Hall on St. Peter Street in the French Quarter. Still the most celebrated jazz club of all, the hall is a remarkably ramshackle old building in which old-time musicians play sets for a reverent audience of jazz aficionados. Equally as famous as its music are New Orleans's restaurants; many of the city's dining establishments are internationally renowned. A specialty is Creole cuisine, a blend of French and Spanish cooking spiced with touches from the West Indies and Africa. Another New Orleans culinary tradition is beignets and cafe au lait at the 200-year-old French Market. The old vegetable market is still in operation; the other market buildings now house an inviting collection of shops, cafes, restaurants and praline makers.

If you enjoy crowds and have a taste for unfettered revelry, come to New Orleans for Mardi Gras! Mardi Gras is French for "Fat Tuesday," or Shrove Tuesday, the day before Lent. The famous celebration, with torchlight parades and street dancing, runs for about two weeks and ends at midnight on Shrove Tuesday. Dozens of private social organizations called Krewes host marvelous costume balls, but unless you know someone in one of the Krewes it's not easy to secure an invitation. Even so, there's lots of fun to be had just watching the parades or

Louisiana

better still, joining in. The entire city goes deliriously insane; the streets are jammed with people; the paraders are outrageously flamboyant; the music, color and excitement are just too contagious to resist.

Guest houses are another old, cherished tradition in New Orleans, and there are many excellent ones to choose from. If you plan to visit during Mardi Gras or for any other special event such as the Sugar Bowl, however, be sure to make reservations well in advance—even a year ahead if possible.

The Lafitte Guest House. The romance of the French Quarter enhances each visit to this charming guest house at the corner of Bourbon and St. Philip streets. Although it is only steps away from all the hustle and bustle of the commercial end of Bourbon Street, Lafitte is in the quiet residential section of the Quarter. An elegant French manor house, the building was erected in 1849 as a single-family dwelling for Paul Joseph Geleises. Carefully restored, the Lafitte today is furnished throughout with magnificent antiques and reproductions. Dr. Robert and Mrs. Claire Guyton, who have owned the house since 1980, are involved in an ongoing refurbishing endeavor, and many of the items of furniture, accessories and oil paintings are from their personal collection.

The ivy-covered main house, with its several wrought-iron balconies graced by hanging plants, contains nine guest rooms. All of the high-ceilinged rooms are extremely spacious, and many feature fireplaces and crystal chandeliers. Some have balconies; others overlook the landscaped courtyard. In addition, there are five guest rooms in the *garçonierre* (slave quarters). These accommodations, which open onto the courtyard, are smaller but equally charming. All of the rooms have private baths and are carpeted, air conditioned and heated. Each is individually decorated and offers either a queen- or king-size bed.

The rates include a continental breakfast of freshly squeezed orange juice, warm croissants or brioche, butter and jam, and New Orleans–style coffee. Breakfast is served in your room on a tray, in the splendid Victorian parlor, or out in the courtyard. All of the attractions in the French Quarter are within walking distance, including Royal Street

Bed & Breakfast

with its world-renowned collection of antique shops. The friendly staff, led by Sam Albright, will be pleased to help with tours, restaurant reservations or anything else you need to make your stay enjoyable, relaxed and memorable.

The Lafitte Guest House, 1003 Bourbon St., New Orleans, LA 70116; (504) 581-2678. Rates are expensive; 10% discount weekdays from June 1 to Aug. 31. The rates are not increased for Mardi Gras, Sugar Bowl games or other special events, but please check for minimum number of nights required at these times. Visa, MasterCard and American Express are accepted. Children are welcome; no pets, please. Off-street parking (a rarity in the French Quarter) is available. Open year-round.

Hotel Maison de Ville. Old World elegance and attentive personal service are the hallmarks of the Maison de Ville, a New Orleans guest house that is in the tradition of the classic small French hotel. Its staff, beginning with Bonnie Leigh, general manager, works hard to assure your every comfort. There is a bellman to take care of cars and a concierge who will book dinner reservations, advise on shopping and arrange sightseeing tours. Beds are turned down each night, and a foil-wrapped chocolate is left on the pillow. Even the nice old custom of shining shoes left outside the bedroom door is still faithfully observed. In the morning, a silver tray bearing freshly squeezed orange juice, croissants, a pot of fragrant New Orleans chicory coffee, tea or hot chocolate, a copy of the *Times-Picayune* and a fresh rose is brought to your door or served in the courtyard or salon. Tea, sherry and port are served every afternoon, and coffee, hot chocolate, fruit, sodas, mixers and ice are available throughout the day. All are *lagniappe* —complimentary.

Maison de Ville and its associated Audubon Cottages date back to the late eighteenth century. The main house is actually a group of buildings constructed as a private home; the original slave quarters are thought to be among the oldest structures in New Orleans. All surround a classic New Orleans courtyard with balconies, stairs, wrought-iron furniture, tropical plants and a charming triple-tiered fountain with a fish pond. The formal downstairs salon with marble fireplaces is furnished with exquisite French accent pieces and antique mirrors. The twelve double rooms and two suites available for guests are furnished in such eighteenth- and nineteenth-century antiques as four posters, marble basins and brass fittings. Some of the accommodations are in the old slave quarters, at the rear of the courtyard. Tennessee Williams, it is said, worked on his play *A Streetcar Named Desire* while staying in room 9. All rooms have private baths.

The seven Audubon Cottages, a block and a half away, also offer accommodations for guests. The cottages, some of which date back to the days of the first Spanish settlers, are clustered around a central courtyard with a swimming pool, behind a 100-year-old stucco wall. They are named for John James Audubon, who resided here with his family in the early 1800s while painting some of his *Birds of America*. The original cottages have been renovated into modern living quarters, and several newer ones in the same Creole style have been added. The decor is cool, spare Spanish with brick walls, brick or tile floors, and ceilings with exposed beams. Each cottage has at least one bedroom, a private bath, a kitchen kept stocked with soft drinks, lemons and mixers, and its own private courtyard and flower garden. All of the services received by guests in the main house are also provided for cottage guests.

Hotel Maison de Ville, 727 Toulouse St., New Orleans, LA 70130; (504) 561-5858; (800) 634-1600. Visa, MasterCard and American Express are accepted. Rates are very expensive. Well-behaved children are welcome; no pets, please. Parking is provided near the hotel at $10.50/day (a bellman assists). Open year-round.

LaMothe House. A stately nineteenth-century mansion, beautifully restored and modernized, LaMothe House is on tree-shaded Esplanade Avenue in the French Quarter. The three-story house was built around 1800 by Jean LaMothe, a wealthy sugar planter of French descent, originally from the West Indies. LaMothe and his family sought refuge in New Orleans after an insurrection in Santo Domingo. Their new home soon became one of the city's most social, echoing with the gaiety and gallantry of aristocratic Creole Louisiana.

LaMothe House was constructed in the French style as one of the city's earliest double townhouses, for two families, with a porte-cochere, or carriageway, through the middle. In 1860, four hand-carved Corinthian columns were added to the double entrance, and the porte-cochere became the main hallway leading to twin winding stairways that sweep up to the second-floor reception area and third-floor suites. The patio still boasts its original flagstones, imported as ships' ballast.

For guests there are six guest rooms opening onto the patio or onto the balcony above, and five suites in the main house. All are furnished

Bed & Breakfast

with authentic antiques, including canopied beds and large armoires, and have private baths (with tub and shower), room telephones, color TV and air conditioning. Except for weekends, daily laundry and dry cleaning services are available. A nice touch is the nightly turn-down service; a praline prepared by LaMothe House is left on the pillow.

In addition, there are guest accommodations in the adjacent Creole Cottage. Built circa 1840, the cypress-framed, four-bay structure is typical of many of the early Creole cottages and homes built within the Faubourg Marigny. The Creoles, descendants of European French and Spanish families, were the first to settle beyond the Vieux Carre. The first faubourg, or subdivision, was laid out in 1805 as the plantation of Bernard de Marigny, who inherited it from his father, Pierre Phillipe de Marigny de Mandeville, in 1800. The cottage, with its original wide floorboards, French doors and shutters, includes two double rooms and two suites, one with fireplace and one with its own private patio; all have private baths.

Complimentary *petit dejéuner*, or "little breakfast," is served to guests each morning in LaMothe House's handsomely appointed dining room: juice, sweet rolls or biscuits, coffee or tea. A lovely 200-year-old Sheffield urn is on display. Afternoon wine and tea are served. The helpful staff, headed by Ms. Susan Gouaux, will assist guests in making dinner reservations and planning tours. The house is within walking distance of the French Quarter's restaurants, shops and historic sites, and guided bus or limousine tours of the city and the bayou country are available, with pickup at the door.

LaMothe House, 621 Esplanade Ave., New Orleans, LA 70116; (504) 947-1161 or 947-1162. Rates are expensive. American Express, Visa and MasterCard are accepted. Children are welcome; no pets, please. Free parking is provided. Open year-round.

The Cornstalk Hotel. One of the French Quarter's most photographed sites, the Cornstalk Hotel is famous for its unique, ornate wrought-iron fence with a delicate cornstalk motif. Behind the fence stands a gracious 200-year-old Victorian mansion, painted white, with tall columns and a gallery. Harriet Beecher Stowe once stayed in the house; reputedly, she was inspired to write *Uncle Tom's Cabin* after witnessing the sights at nearby slave markets. An early 1830s owner, Judge François Xavier-Martin, was the author of the first history of Louisiana, a formulator of that state's civil code, Louisiana's first Supreme Court Chief Justice, and a friend and counsel to Andrew Jackson. The house has been used in numerous movies and is listed in the National Register of Historic Places.

Now elegantly restored, the Cornstalk Hotel is owned by Mr. and Mrs. D. Spencer. They have fourteen rooms for guests, each with a private bath: all are beautifully appointed with antiques. Six of the rooms are on the ground floor. Continental breakfast, included in the rates, consists of juice, freshly baked croissants, coffee or tea. Breakfast,

Louisiana

accompanied by a morning newspaper, is served on the front gallery, patio or direct to your room.

The Cornstalk Hotel, 915 Royal St., New Orleans, LA 70116; (504) 523-1515. Rates are expensive, increased for Mardi Gras and other special events; children are free. No pets, please. Limited parking is available. Open year-round.

Soniat House. Joseph Soniat Dufossat was a prosperous plantation owner who built Soniat House in 1829 as a townhouse for his large family. Today, your host, Rodney R. Smith, has restored the house, with meticulous attention to detail and retaining its architectural integrity. There is an ambiance of luxury throughout: furnishings are of English, French and American antiques, bedsteads were hand-carved, custom fabrics adorn every room, antique Oriental rugs cover the hardwood floors, and works by New Orleans artists adorn the walls. There are twenty-three guest rooms available, all with private baths. Nine are located on the ground floor. Blended with the old-world charm are modern conveniences—bath-side telephones, special soaps, luxurious bed linens, extra reading pillows and an evening turn-down service. There are also Jacuzzi baths in several rooms.

You will enjoy the complimentary breakfast either in the privacy of your room, on your balcony or by the lily pond in the garden. Rich Creole coffee, homemade preserves with biscuits, and freshly squeezed orange juice is served on glowing silver. Other special amenities include a limousine service to the business district each morning and concierge service for travel arrangements, restaurant reservations, theater tickets and picnic baskets for plantation outings. From your location in the heart of the French Quarter, guests are within walking distance of some of New Orleans' best restaurants and shops.

The Soniat House, 1133 Chartres St., New Orleans, LA 70116; (504) 522-0570. Rates are expensive, with lower rates for off season (June 15–Aug. 28). Ameri-

Bed & Breakfast

can Express, Visa and MasterCard are accepted. Children are welcome; no pets, please. Parking available at the house. Open year-round.

Terrell House. Located in the historic lower garden district, Terrell House was built circa 1858 by Richard Terrell, a wealthy cotton merchant and cotton press owner. The Historic New Orleans Collection archive has the original building plans and contract on file. The exterior of the house is an adaptation of the Greek Revival style. Inside are three main floors furnished in period antiques, Oriental carpets and gaslight chandeliers. In addition to the main building, the original kitchen and servants' quarters have been converted to use as guest rooms. The owner, Frederick H. Nicaud, and resident managers, Stephen and Diana Young, have ten elegant guest rooms, decorated with antique ante-bellum furnishings, including tester beds, marble mantels and table tops, and gold mirrors. Ten-foot-tall windows open onto balconies which overlook the courtyard. Two guest rooms are on the ground floor, and all rooms have private baths. Modern conveniences, in each room, include color TV, AM-FM radio, telephone, and central air conditioning and heat.

Included in the rates is a continental breakfast which includes rice callas (an old family recipe), muffins, biscuits, fruit, Creole chicory coffee and tea. At the end of the day, complimentary evening cocktails are served. By prior arrangement, the Youngs will prepare a dinner of Creole specialties: seafood filé gumbo, poulet sauté, Creole tomatoes (in season) with basil sauce, fresh-baked French bread and dessert.

Guests are welcome to enjoy the large, double parlor for reading and relaxing, and the dining room and kitchen are also available. The courtyard provides a peaceful respite. In addition to a giant crape myrtle which is over 125 years old, the courtyard has lush vegetation and flowering plants. Your hosts will arrange tours of New Orleans and its environs. Within a few blocks of the Terrell House are unique gift, antique and art shops, and some of the city's finest restaurants

Mississippi

Creamy blossoms in the spring, pretty girls in hoopskirts welcoming visitors to white-columned ante-bellum mansions, cotton fields and Civil War battlegrounds—Mississippi offers them all, in abundance. Called the Magnolia State, Mississippi is just as romantically Deep South as its nickname implies. But the state is far from being a living monument to the past. Modern industry thrives in Mississippi, as does agriculture. Today, however, soybeans have supplanted cotton as the major cash crop.

Much of the state's early history is shared with that of neighboring Louisiana. Hernando de Soto explored the region in the mid-1500s, discovering the Mississippi River. Robert Cavelier, Sieur de La Salle, claimed the entire river valley for France in 1682 and named it Louisiana in honor of Louis XIV. In 1699, Pierre Lemoyne, Sieur de Iberville, brought a band of colonists from France and founded Biloxi. Lemoyne's brother, Jean Baptiste, established Mississippi's second French settlement at Fort Rosalie (later Natchez) in 1716; two years later he founded New Orleans.

France ceded its territory east of the Mississippi River, except for New Orleans, to England in 1763. The upper Mississippi region became part of the Georgia colony, the lower area part of British West Florida. During the American Revolution, while the British were busy trying to hang on to their northern colonies, the Spanish seized West Florida. In 1798, the United States government created the Mississippi Territory, which included part of present-day Mississippi and Alabama. The territory was later extended north to the Tennessee border and, after American settlers took part of West Florida away from Spain in 1810, it was extended south to the Gulf of Mexico. In 1817, the Mississippi Territory was divided: Alabama became a separate territory, and Mississippi joined the Union as its twentieth state.

Mississippi prospered in the years before the Civil War. Great cotton plantations brought enormous wealth to their owners; most of the state's beautiful historic homes were built during that era. Mississippi seceded from the Union on Jan. 9, 1861, and during the Civil War years was the scene of many fierce battles and skirmishes. The state was readmitted to the Union in 1870, but some twenty years passed before Mississippi really began to recover from the disastrous effects of the war and its immediate aftermath.

Bed & Breakfast

Southern Mississippi

Biloxi, on the Gulf of Mexico, is a charming old town. A popular year-round resort since the mid-1800s, it is renowned for its superb sport fishing, a twenty-six-mile beach and a warm, semi-tropical climate that causes camellias, roses and magnolias to bloom even in winter. Visitors may tour Beauvoir, last home of Confederate President Jefferson Davis. The house, gardens and grounds have been restored, and original Davis family furniture and personal possessions are on view.

Deer Island, half a mile offshore, was once a stopping-off place for pirates. Legend claims that some of their ill-gotten treasure was buried here. Ship Island, twelve miles out, offers excellent surf fishing and swimming. The British used the island as a base for their fleet when they attacked New Orleans in 1815. During summer months visitors may tour an old fort; partly constructed just before the Civil War, the fort was occupied both by Confederate and Federal forces.

Hattiesburg to the north is the home of the University of Southern Mississippi and adjoins the 500,420-acre De Soto National Forest. Over to the west, where the Mississippi River separates the state from Louisiana, travelers will find the start of the famous Natchez Trace. One of Mississippi's greatest attractions, the historic Trace, originally an ancient Indian wilderness trail, is now a scenic parkway maintained by the National Park Service. A few sections are not yet completed, but when they are the road will extend for 447 miles, running diagonally across Mississippi northeast from Natchez, through a portion of Alabama and then into southern Tennessee and up to Nashville.

Historic markers along the way tell the romantic story of the Trace, indicating remnants of the original trail and pointing to various exhibits and nearby places of interest. Indian mounds, village sites and shell heaps offer evidence that the Trace was regularly used as early as 8000 years ago. When white people came, they also followed the old trail, and by the early 1800s the Natchez Trace had become the most heavily traveled road in the Old Southwest. Settlers seeking homesteads traversed its length; post riders carried the mail along its course; Gen. Andrew Jackson and his soldiers walked the Trace to and from the Battle of New Orleans. Goods were floated down the Mississippi on flatboats to Natchez or New Orleans; the return journey was made overland via the trail. Outlaws, too, used the Natchez Trace, preying on innocent travelers.

Natchez/Lorman

Natchez, at the southwestern end of the Natchez Trace and probably Mississippi's most visited town, is one of the oldest settlements in the state. The Natchez Indians, for whom the town is named, hunted buffalo and worshipped sun gods here for generations before the first Europeans came. In 1682, the French explorer La Salle discovered the bluffs of Natchez and realized that whoever controlled the heights would also control the river. Fort Rosalie was built on the site in 1716. The Natchez Indians accepted the newcomers peaceably enough until 1729, when they massacred the entire French garrison. The French quickly took revenge and chased the Indians out of the region. After the end of the French and Indian Wars Natchez came under British control, which lasted until the American Revolution, when it was seized by the Spanish. In 1798, the United States took over the town as part of the Mississippi Territory.

Natchez today prides itself on being "a museum of the Old South" with a splendid collection of nearly 100 ante-bellum mansions and plantation houses. The imposing structures, with such beguiling names as Airlie, Mistletoe, Mount Repose, Green Leaves and Ravenna, all have a story to tell. During the town's annual Pilgrimage tours, held in the spring and fall, more than 30 of these homes are open to the public for viewing. About 15 of the grand Greek Revival mansions are open year-round as well; ask for information at the Chamber of Commerce, 300 N. Commerce St. A growing number of Natchez houses also offer overnight accommodations to travelers.

By the river at the bottom of the bluffs, visitors will find Natchez-Under-the-Hill. This area, now restored and offering several shops, pubs and restaurants, was originally a notoriously rowdy hell-hole much favored by river travelers as a place to drink, gamble, find a less-than-ladylike woman and most likely have an enjoyable fight or two. Another interesting site in the Natchez area is the Grand Village of the Natchez Indians, with a museum, nature trails, archeological digs and a slide show.

At Jefferson College (no longer a school), three miles east of town, you may explore the church where Aaron Burr was arraigned for treason in 1807. Flat-topped Emerald Mound, twelve miles northeast of Natchez, extends over eight acres and is the third largest Indian mound in the United States. Constructed by Mississippi Indians about 600 years ago, the mound was designed as a base for ceremonial buildings, not for burial purposes. Historic Springfield Plantation, where Andrew Jackson was married, is twenty miles northeast near Fayette. Built between 1786 and 1790, the house contains the original mantelpieces and woodwork, along with displays of Civil War and railroad memorabilia. Over on the other side of the Mississippi, in Louisiana's St. Francisville region, are many more picturesque old plantations.

The Burn. Back in the nineteenth century a young man named John P. Walworth was traveling down the Mississippi by steamboat, on his way to New Orleans to seek his fortune. During a stopover at Natchez, however, Walworth found the town so appealing that he decided to

Bed & Breakfast

stay. He built the Burn around 1832, naming it for a small brook, or "burn" in Scottish, that once flowed through the property. During the Civil War the Burn was occupied by Union troops, who used it as their headquarters and then turned it into a federal hospital.

The house, which was completely restored in the 1970s, is now owned by Tony and Loveta Byrne. (Tony has served as mayor of Natchez for the past eighteen years.) There are six spacious rooms for guests, all furnished with lovely antiques and offering private baths, TV and air conditioning. Each of the rooms accommodates two or more persons. Guests are, of course, given a tour of the house, which is fronted by four white columns and a broad piazza. Brick steps lead up the sloping lawn to the wide front door. A few of the

Burn's many outstanding features are the graceful semi-spiral, free-standing stairway in the entrance hall, originally a carriageway, and the Victorian music room with hand-carved furnishings, Sevres porcelain and several musical instruments.

Comfortable chairs on the piazza provide a cool place to sit and look out over the lawn, with its tall shade trees, lush shrubbery and flowers. The Burn is noted for its gardens, including splendidly planted terraces and an old-fashioned, walled herb garden with a handsome fountain. A swimming pool, at the rear of the house above the terraces, is available for a refreshing dip. Arriving guests are welcomed with a complimentary glass of wine, and an ample plantation-style breakfast is also included in the rates. Served in the

Mississippi

formal dining room, appointed with matching Regency servers, breakfast may include freshly squeezed orange juice in pewter goblets, ham and eggs and grits, biscuits and jam, and excellent coffee. In the afternoon, refreshments are offered in the elegant downstairs parlor. The Burn is within easy walking distance of several good restaurants, the Mississippi River, Natchez-Under-the-Hill and many other historic houses.

The Burn, 712 N. Union St., Natchez, MS 39120; (601) 445-8566 or 442-1344. Rates are expensive. Visa and MasterCard are accepted. No children under school age, please, and no pets. Parking is available on the grounds. Open year-round except Christmas and New Year's.

Texada. The first brick house in Natchez, Texada, built in 1792, is situated downtown in the Old Spanish Quarter. Don Manuel Texada, for whom the house is named, lived there between 1797 and 1817.

Over the years the building has served as a tavern, hotel and Territorial Legislative Hall. Containing a fine collection of American and English period furnishings, the house, now in the National Register of Historic Places and included on Pilgrimage tours, is owned by Dr. and Mrs. George W. Moss. For guests there are four double rooms, all with private baths, opening into the upstairs living room, which has a TV and telephone. A hearty Southern-style breakfast, included in the rates, offers fruit juice, choice of cereals, ham, bacon or sausage, eggs, grits and hot muffins.

Texada, 222 S. Wall St., Natchez, MS 39120; (601) 445-4283. Rates are expensive. Children older than 3 are welcome; no pets, please. On-street parking is available. Open year-round, but advance reservations are requested.

Silver Street Inn. Another of Natchez's large collection of historic buildings, the Silver Street Inn is unique in that it is located on the

Bed & Breakfast

river, down in Natchez-Under-the-Hill. A narrow strip of land below the city's bluffs, Natchez-Under-the-Hill was the most notorious region in the South back in the early and mid-1800s. Inhabited by hard-drinking, brawling boatmen and trappers, gamblers and prostitutes, the area more than earned its bad reputation. So evil were some of its denizens that many of the town's residents believed they alone precipitated the earthquake of 1811! But times have changed, and Natchez-Under-the-Hill is no longer the sordid riverport it was. Today the area is amiable and safe, with restaurants and shops where gambling houses, saloons and brothels once roared with drunken debauches and riots. And Silver Street Inn, a disreputable "bawdy house" of the 1840s, is now a homey, comfortable guest house.

Owner Lu Barraza, who opened the inn in 1980, thinks that the building may have belonged to a famous Natchez woman, the red-haired Madam Aivoges. Legend has it that the glamorous madam, who managed to keep her background a mystery, had a son. The boy, who was also kept in the dark concerning his mother's occupation, came to Natchez one day unexpectedly, on vacation from his exclusive Eastern school. He believed that his mother lived on a plantation somewhere in the area; he did not expect to find her running the most celebrated brothel on the waterfront. When the two met, the young man was so horrified that he fired his pistol at her heart, killing her on the spot.

Ms. Barraza says the house is now inhabited by a friendly ghost who, she believes, may have been a prostitute. When footsteps are heard, it seems to be more than one person. Occasionally, the ghost likes to lie down on a bed, leaving an impression when no one has been in the room!

Now charmingly restored, the Silver Street Inn offers four rooms for guests, one of which is actually a two-bedroom suite. They're all upstairs; the lower level of the building is a specialty shop for fine ladies' apparel, operated by your hostess. Guests enter by an outside stairway into a "keeping room" furnished in country antiques. The cozy room includes a wood-burning fireplace, with plenty of extra firewood, TV, and warm touches of brass and copper. The individually decorated guest rooms, done in Robin Red and Confederate Blue, are furnished with simple country pieces including tester and iron beds, armoires and old chests. Braided rugs cover the hardwood floors, and nutmeg-scented candles fill the air with fragrance. Two of the rooms open onto the upper gallery overlooking Silver Street and the river. The two-bedroom suite and another bedroom have private baths; the other two bedrooms share a bath.

A complimentary crock of wine will be found in each room, and a continental breakfast of juice, coffee and Silver Street's own bran muffins is also included in the rates. Guests make their own breakfast in the modern kitchen—where the refrigerator contains the batter for the delectable, raisiny muffins, all ready to be baked. In addition to the keeping room there are the balcony, with rocking chairs, and an enclosed courtyard in the rear of the building for relaxing.

Silver Street Inn, 1 Silver St., P. O. Box 1224, Natchez, MS 39120; (601) 442-4221. (At the end of Main, State or Jefferson streets, follow along the bluff on Broadway to Silver Street. Go down the hill; the inn is the first building on the left.) Rates are moderately expensive. American Express, Visa, MasterCard and Diner's Club are accepted. Children and pets are welcome. Parking is available. Open year-round.

Linden. Used in the filming of *Gone With the Wind*, Linden (circa 1800) is an architectural treasure from the Federal period. Mrs. Jeanette S. Feltus, your gracious hostess, says that the house has been in her family since 1849, and her children are the sixth generation to live there. The property was originally granted to Madam Sarah Truly by the King of Spain in 1785. Throughout the house are eighteenth- and nineteenth-century antiques, many of them family heirlooms: crystal from France, porcelain from China, American and English period pieces. There are also, according to Mrs. Feltus, several family ghosts—all friendly!

Bed & Breakfast

For guests there are seven tastefully decorated double and triple bedrooms, all with private baths. Three of the rooms are on the ground floor. For relaxing, there is Linden's spacious rear gallery, with rocking chairs, a ceiling fan, a telephone and TV. A tour of the house and a full Southern breakfast of orange juice, eggs, ham and grits, homemade biscuits, coffee or tea are included in the rates. Breakfast is served on the back gallery. You will need a car to reach restaurants, shops, and other historic Natchez homes.

Linden, 1 Linden Place, Natchez, MS 39120; (601) 445-5472. Rates are expensive. Children over 12 are welcome; no pets, please, and no loud parties or unruly conduct. Parking is available. Open year-round.

Elgin Plantation. A typical nineteenth-century Southern plantation home, Elgin is a spacious frame building with wide upper and lower galleries supported by slender Doric columns. The land was deeded to Carlos White as a Spanish grant in the late 1700s; part of the basement fireplace of his original cottage still remains. Dr. John Carmichael Jenkins purchased the property in the late 1830s for his bride, Annis Dunbar, whose family owned the adjoining plantation. Elgin was named for the Scottish birthplace of Sir William Dunbar.

The front or main section of the house was built around 1839 and added on to in later years. Dr. Jenkins, a pioneer horticulturist as well as a medical doctor, planted a magnificent collection of trees and flowers, including an orchard, boxwood and camellia bushes, and some fifty magnolias. The magnolias, along with moss-draped live oak trees, create a splendid picture for visitors approaching the house. In the spring, azaleas, purple wisteria, yellow jasmine and blossoming redbud add their own beauty to the scene.

The house, now owned by Dr. and Mrs. William F. Calhoun, is furnished throughout with American and English antiques and Oriental rugs. A center hall features a graceful stairway with a cherry newelpost, rail and turned balusters. The library includes a group of Piranesi etchings, and the dining room is highlighted by a punkah, an oak fan suspended above the table. Before screens were invented, the hand-pulled fan was used to keep flies away.

Guests at Elgin stay in a separate two-story structure behind the main house. Built in 1853 as a dependency to the main house, it was used as slave quarters until after the Civil War, then as living quarters for the plantation's overseers. Constructed of brick, the guest house is fronted by four white columns and has both an upper and lower gallery. Downstairs there are a large living room and dining room, a half bath and fully equipped kitchen. Upstairs are a two-bedroom suite and bath with shower and tub, and a one-bedroom suite with a bath and shower. All bedrooms include one double and one twin bed. The attractive accommodations are furnished in late nineteenth-century period pieces.

Guests are offered a tour of the main house and a full Southern

Mississippi

breakfast of ham, grits, homemade biscuits and Elgin wild plum jelly, included in the rates. A pot of hot coffee is available at an early hour for guests who rise before breakfast is ready.

Elgin Plantation, Rte. 3, Natchez, MS 39120; (601) 446-6100. (Turn off Rte. 61 South 3 miles from city limits at Elgin sign and follow paved road for 1 mile.) Rates are expensive, lower for longer stays. Children are welcome; no pets, please. The guest house has its own private drive and parking. Open year-round.

Oakland Plantation. Andrew Jackson's wife-to-be, Rachel Robards, was once a guest at Oakland. Today, Mr. and Mrs. Andrew Peabody offer Natchez-style Southern hospitality to their guests. The main house, built in 1821 and added to in 1831, contains many beautiful early English and American pieces, paintings and prints. The plantation's original house, now the guest quarters, was constructed in 1792 of native brick. Furnished with antiques and reproductions, it features large fireplaces once used for cooking and the original mantels.

There are three double bedrooms for guests, one on the ground floor, and two baths—one shared and one private. A lounge (with TV), a kitchenette and a dining area are also available for guests' use, and breakfast of juice, bacon, eggs, cereal, toast and coffee is included in the rates. Guests are given a tour of the main house and are welcome to explore Oakland's 360 acres, with several fishing ponds, trail walks

and game preserves. There's a tennis court, too, which visitors may use.

Oakland Plantation, Rte. 3, Box 203, Natchez, MS 39120; toll free (800) 647-6746 or (601) 445-5101. (Seven miles south of Natchez.) Rates are moderately expensive, lower for longer stays. Children over 10 are welcome; no pets, please. Parking is available. Open year-round.

Rosswood Plantation. Easily located from the Natchez Trace, heading north toward Vicksburg, is this quintessential Southern mansion,

Bed & Breakfast

Rosswood. Present owners Jean and Walt Hylander invite guests to come and share their unique and captivating cameo of the Old South which spreads out over a 100-acre rural setting. Guests will enjoy reading a journal kept by the first owner of Rosswood, Dr. Walter W. Wade. It tells of everyday life on a cotton plantation and gives insights into Southern society and the business affairs of a physician/planter 120 years ago. Guests can also read an eyewitness account of a slave revolt which took place in the area as a result of a contested will which negated their freedom. Records indicate that during the Civil War, wounded from both sides were brought to Rosswood for treatment. A Union officer is said to have died there and been buried in an unidentified grave on the grounds. This story has spawned the legend of a "friendly ghost" who sometimes greets occupants with a cheerful "Hello!"

The mansion was also formerly owned by Elizabeth Hamer, favorite niece of Jefferson Davis; however, during the 1930s, the house was home to four sharecropper families and was saved from deterioration and destruction by Mr. and Mrs. Daniel Mason and then further improved by Mr. and Mrs. Douglas Black. Rosswood is listed in the National Register of Historic Places.

A classic Greek Revival structure, Rosswood was built in 1857 by David Shroder, who was the architect of Windsor, a magnificent mansion in Claiborne County, destroyed by fire in 1890. Col. and Mrs. Hylander have gone to great lengths to restore the home and have filled it with period Victorian antiques. Additional restoration is being carried out under guidance from the Department of Archives and History of the State of Mississippi. There are four guest rooms available, none on the ground floor; two have private baths. Guests can enjoy coffee and juice served in their rooms, and a full plantation breakfast is available. Guests may use the parlor and library, and they will also enjoy the gallery with its spectacular view of the formal gardens and grounds. Guided tours are available for those travelers not staying at Rosswood.

Rosswood Plantation, Lorman, MS 39096; (601) 437-4215. (Just off US-61. At Lorman, the Old Country Store and the yellow blinking light, turn east toward Red Lick, Rte. 552. At about 2½ miles, watch for Rosswood on left.) Rates are expensive. Visa and MasterCard are accepted. Children are welcome; no pets, please. Parking available at the house. Open year-round.

Central Mississippi

Vicksburg/Port Gibson

Jackson, Mississippi's capital, is northeast of Natchez, just a short distance from the Natchez Trace. Named for Andrew Jackson, the city sits atop high bluffs overlooking the Pearl River. During the Civil War, most of the town was burned by General Sherman's troops. Jackson, home of the Mississippi State Fair, held each October, is also famed for the Spring Pilgrimage during which many of the city's lovely old houses and gardens are open to the public. The Mississippi State Historical Society in the Old Capitol Building offers dioramas and exhibits tracing the state's history. A handsome Greek Revival structure, the building was begun in 1833 and completely restored in the late 1950s. The new State Capitol, built in 1903, is a replica of our nation's capitol in Washington, D.C., and the exterior of the Governor's Mansion resembles the White House.

West of Jackson, Vicksburg was another scene of Civil War strife. In June, 1862, the town was held by the Confederates. Their batteries, situated on bluffs above the Mississippi River, were in excellent position to fire upon Northern forces trying to move up or down the river. Gen. Ulysses S. Grant was determined to take the town; after several attempts to storm it failed, he decided to surround the place and starve it into submission. The siege lasted for forty-seven days. Vicksburg's inhabitants dug caves in which to hide from the almost constant barrage of cannon and mortar fire. But the lack of incoming supplies took its toll, and starvation became a reality. The Confederate forces surrendered the town on July 4. Although the war continued for two more years, many historians feel that the Southern cause was lost forever at Vicksburg. Today Vicksburg's location makes it a center of trade and commerce.

At the Old Court House Museum, where Grant raised the U.S. flag after capturing the town, visitors will find an interesting collection of Civil War, pioneer and Indian artifacts. Vicksburg National Military Park and Cemetery, with a sixteen-mile self-guided tour, runs along the eastern and northern edges of the city.

Civil War buffs may also want to visit Tupelo National Battlefield, north of Jackson on the Natchez Trace. Here a Union force led by generals A. J. Smith and Joseph A. Mower met Confederate Gen. Nathan Bedford Forrest in an engagement on July 14, 1864. Although the outcome was inconclusive, the Confederate troops were prevented from taking the railroad, which General Sherman needed to mount his campaign against Atlanta. To the west is Oxford, named for the renowned English university town and home of the University of Mississippi. Rowan Oaks, the home of Nobel Prize-winner William Faulkner, is here, and the area includes many of Faulkner's fictional Yoknapatawpha County landmarks.

Anchuca. Originally this stately mansion was a one-level wood structure built by J. W. Mauldin around 1830. Around 1840, Mr. Mauldin, a selectman on the Vicksburg Governing Board, added what was described as a "pretentious front" on the house: part of the front wood structure was shaved off to accommodate the elaborate Greek Revival facade. In addition to the extensively restored main house, slave

Bed & Breakfast

quarters and a turn-of-the-century cottage have been redone to provide additional guest rooms. Anchuca is in the historic district of Vicksburg, and records indicate that Jefferson Davis once made a speech from Anchuca's balcony.

Your hosts, May and Martin White, have carefully selected all the decorations, which are period antiques and artifacts. Weary travelers will enjoy resting under canopied beds. There are nine rooms, six on the ground floor, and all have private baths. Guests may use the library in the main house, and there is a swimming pool with Jacuzzi in the indoor/outdoor cabana. Included in the rates is a full "plantation" breakfast of juice, coffee, hot biscuits, cheese grits, scrambled eggs, bacon and pancakes, most of which is homemade. This fare is served in the magnificent formal dining room under the gaslit chandelier. Also gratis is a "Julep" party: guests sip mint juleps or wine from pewter cups in the lush herb garden.

Anchuca, 1010 First East, Vicksburg, MS 39180; (601) 636-4931; outside MS, (800) 262-4822. (Exit 4-B down Clay Street to 8th stoplight; right on Cherry Street. Go 5 blocks to First East; turn right.) Rates are expensive, with lower rates off season, Dec. 1–Feb. 28. American Express, Visa and MasterCard are accepted. Children and pets are welcome. Parking available at the house. Open year-round.

Oak Square. Port Gibson, the city that Gen. Ulysses S. Grant said was "too beautiful to burn," is the setting for Oak Square, named for the massive oak trees surrounding the property. Oak Square is Port Gibson's largest and most palatial mansion. Built circa 1850 by a cotton planter, Oak Square is on the National Register of Historic Places and in Mississippi's First National Historic District. Mr. and Mrs. William

Mississippi

Lum, owners and hosts, have recently restored the mansion to its original elegance. The exterior is Greek Revival style surrounded by a courtyard, fountain and gazebo. Inside, there are eight suites, one on the ground floor, and all with private baths. Furnishings are period antiques, and guests sleep in canopied beds from the eighteenth and nineteenth centuries. Modern conveniences include color TV and air conditioning as well as a chairlift to the upstairs rooms. Of special interest to visitors is a rare collection of Civil War memorabilia, including many original family documents and a Confederate sword belonging to Maj. R. C. McCay, Mr. Lum's great-grandfather. Guests may use two large sitting rooms in the main house. Included in the rates is a guided tour of the mansion and grounds, as well as a full Southern breakfast: Southern grits; home-cured ham, bacon or sausage; scrambled eggs; homemade biscuits with jelly and preserves; orange juice and fresh fruit, in season; and coffee or tea. Upon arrival, guests are offered wine and cheese.

Activities in the area include tours of historic homes and churches, the Grand Gulf Military Park with Civil War forts and museum, and the ruins of Windsor, one of the most palatial homes in the South, which was destroyed by fire in 1890.

Oak Square, 1207 Church St., Port Gibson, MS 39150; (601) 437-4350, 437-5771 or 437-5300. (Located on US-61 between Natchez and Vicksburg, 1 mile off the Natchez Trace Parkway.) Rates are moderately expensive, with special

Bed & Breakfast

rates for children. American Express, Visa and MasterCard are accepted. Children are welcome; no pets, please (a kennel is located nearby). No smoking in guest bedrooms (only in designated areas). Off-street parking available. Open year-round.

Northern Mississippi

Holly Springs

North of Oxford you'll come to Holly Springs, a pretty town set amid the rolling hills of northern Mississippi near the Tennessee border. In April, Holly Springs opens ten of its lovely ante-bellum homes to visitors. Nearby, the Holly Springs National Forest offers 143,567 acres for hiking, swimming, hunting and fishing.

Hamilton Place. Built in 1838 by William F. Mason, treasurer of the Illinois Central Railroad, Hamilton Place was the scene of a fascinating story. Be sure to have your hosts, Linda and Jack Stubbs, tell how the then owner, Maria Mason, helped save the city of Holly Springs during the Civil War with her Steinway piano!

Restored by the Stubbs in 1976, the home is a typical Louisiana raised cottage and is listed on the National Register of Historic Places. Guests will enjoy the wide veranda with old-fashioned rocking chairs. The house is filled with eighteenth- and nineteenth-century antiques. One guest room has a four-poster tester bed, and another is furnished

Mississippi

in Louis XVI antiques. All three guest rooms are on the ground floor and have private bathrooms. Guests may choose the formal dining room, the veranda or the gazebo as the location of their complimentary breakfast. The fare includes juice, coffee, fresh fruit in season, sausage and egg casserole, and homemade breads. Not recommended for dieters are Hamilton Place's famous angel biscuits with strawberry or honey-lemon butter. In the late afternoon, guests may relax over a wine or cocktail, compliments of the Stubbs. For recreation, there is a seasonal swimming pool or a year-round hot tub. Bikes are also available. Hamilton Place's former carriage house has been transformed into the Copper Fish Antique Shop. Guests will enjoy special tours through historic Holly Springs which has an abundance of ante-bellum homes and churches, an art gallery, a museum, antique shops, and the 1837 Hillcrest Cemetery. Also, Hamilton Place is only three blocks from the town square where there are restaurants and shopping.

Hamilton Place, 105 E. Mason Ave., Holly Springs, MS 38635; (601) 252-4368. (Take Holly Springs/Oxford exit off US-78, then look for signs.) Rates are moderately expensive with special rates for longer stays. Visa and MasterCard are accepted. Children are welcome, but no pets, please. Parking available at the house. Open year-round.

North Carolina

New Englanders, on the whole, tend to believe that their six-state region is the most beautiful, varied and historic in the East (if not the entire country). North Carolinians, however, know very well that *their* state—all by itself—offers tough competition. North Carolina's mountains include many peaks higher than those in New England. Mt. Mitchell is, in fact, the highest point east of the Mississippi River. Through these mountains runs one of the country's most spectacular roads, the Blue Ridge Parkway. The state's seacoast, though not as dramatically rock-bound as New England's, offers broad beaches, sand dunes, narrow islands and barrier reefs. Every inch of the coast is saturated with history—the tale of a lost colony, reams of romantic pirate lore, sinister legends of ships lured to their doom and the site of the Wright brothers' first flight.

Even in the matter of chronological firsts, North Carolina comes off a winner: the state's earliest English colony predated the Pilgrims' landing in Massachusetts by thirty-five years. As for weather, North Carolina boasts a delightfully benign climate year-round. Yet (making matters worse) some of the best winter skiing in the East may be enjoyed nowadays on North Carolina's slopes! It's all enough to make a native New Englander choke on his or her baked beans and brown bread.

North Carolina's intriguing story begins with an unsolved mystery. In 1584, Sir Walter Raleigh sent English explorers to investigate the southeastern coast of North America. They reported favorably on the region, and a colonizing mission was dispatched the following year. That first colony was established on Roanoke Island, in what is now North Carolina. It was abandoned a year later, but in 1587 a second group of colonists arrived, led by John White. His granddaughter, Virginia Dare, was the first child of English parents to be born in America.

White sailed back to England for supplies, but because of problems with the Spanish Armada, he and his shipload of goods were unable to set sail again for America until 1590. Upon arrival, White discovered to his dismay that the entire colony—every last soul—had vanished. All that was left was a fort-like enclosure and the word *Croatan* (the name of a friendly local Indian tribe) carved on a post. Because there

Bed & Breakfast

was no evidence of a violent attack or fire, White was forced to believe that the colonists had all gone off to join the Indians. The puzzle remains to this day; although many theories have been put forth, no trace of those lost colonists has ever been found.

One might think that the terrors and hardships of the New World would have caused England to give up the idea of colonizing the land. But tales of its riches continued to spark the acquisitive interest of the crown, and in 1607 the first permanent English colony in America was settled in Jamestown, Virginia. In 1663, Charles II granted the territory south of Virginia to eight Lords Proprietors, who named it Carolina in honor of the king. The huge tract was divided into North Carolina and South Carolina in 1710; eighteen years later the proprietors sold their rights back to the crown, and the Carolinas became royal colonies, each ruled by a royal governor appointed by the king.

The citizens of both Carolinas were, from the start, a free-thinking lot. Most were emigrants from England, Scotland, Ireland and Germany who crossed the Atlantic in search of a new life and who scorned repression of any kind. All hardy individualists, they made the proprietary and royal colony years turbulent ones for their rulers. In April, 1776, North Carolina was the first colony to vote for independence in the American Revolution. Although the British tried to retain their hold over the feisty ex-colonists, they were forced out completely after losing several battles.

North Carolina once again showed its independent nature at the start of the Civil War by being the last state to secede from the Union. Once involved, however, it fought hard. Some 40,000 North Carolinians were killed in the war, the highest number lost by any Confederate state.

Geographically, North Carolina has three distinct regions: the coastal plain and offshore islands, the Piedmont or midlands, and the mountains. Each region contains a multitude of places to see and things to do for vacationers. Those whose tastes run to history will find battlegrounds, exciting historical drama and charming old towns with fascinating pasts. For scenery buffs, the state offers a remarkably diverse choice of attractions: ocean beaches, winding mountain roads with breathtaking vistas at every turn, hillsides blooming with rhododendron and mountain laurel in the spring and flaming with startling color in the fall, freshwater lakes, great rivers, tumbling streams and vast green forests.

Collectors of native crafts will be delighted with the state's wealth of unique handmade items, and the sports-minded will enjoy swimming, boating, fishing and hunting, hiking and horseback riding, skiing and superb golf. The North Carolinians themselves are unpretentiously friendly and very hospitable, with a wickedly dry sense of humor.

North Carolina

Coastal Region

The Outer Banks

A visit to North Carolina should include a drive along the Outer Banks, part of the chain of long, narrow islands and sandy reefs that stretches in a 325-mile curve along the coastline. Before starting out, however, you might enjoy a side trip to historic Edenton on Albemarle Sound; from Elizabeth City follow Route 17 southwest. Edenton has been called North Carolina's prettiest town. Once a prosperous seaport, it is now a dreamy old community with tree-shaded streets and many eighteenth- and nineteenth-century houses. In spring, the town's gardens bloom with jonquils, roses, irises, lilies and tulips.

Edenton's first settlers arrived in 1658. The town was incorporated in 1722 and became the first capital of the province of North Carolina. Several noted Revolutionary patriots lived here, and during the Revolution local exporters defied British blockades by sending desperately needed supplies to Washington's army. In 1774, the ladies of Edenton staged their own Tea Party. In the earliest known instance of political action by American women, fifty-one of them signed a resolution supporting the acts of the rebellious provincial congress. They declared that until the hated British taxes were abolished, they would drink no more tea, nor would they wear English clothing.

To reach the Outer Banks from Edenton, retrace your route back to Elizabeth City and then take Route 158 east and south. Or, you may follow routes 32 and 37 down to Route 64, which will take you east to Roanoke Island and the Fort Raleigh Historic Site. The area in which the lost English colony was located has been excavated, and the fort has been reconstructed to appear as it was when the colonists built it. A Pulitzer Prize–winning historical drama, *The Lost Colony*, graphically and movingly portrays the incredibly hard life those early settlers had to endure. Performed nightly, except Sundays, from late June through August, the production has been running since 1937.

Kill Devil Hills/Ocracoke

From Roanoke Island it is a short drive east and north to Kill Devil Hills, just south of Kitty Hawk. Here you can visit the Wright Brothers National Memorial, site of the famed brothers' first powered airplane flight in 1903. A full-scale replica of the original plane is on view. Farther south, you will come to the popular resort area of Nags Head. Its odd name is derived from the villainous method of wrecking ships practiced long ago, according to legend, by some of the local inhabitants. They would wait for a dark, moonless night, then hang lanterns from the necks of horses and walk them along the dunes. Ships

Bed & Breakfast

making their way along the coast would become confused by the lights and run aground on the dangerous shoals; their cargoes were then "salvaged" by the wily thieves.

Cape Hatteras National Seashore begins at Whalebone Junction, a short distance south of Nags Head. A hard-surface road, Route 12, runs for seventy miles along the seashore; Hatteras Inlet is crossed via a free auto ferry. The seashore is a shifting, always changing region of sand dunes and marshes, dotted with the skeletons of wrecked sailing ships. If you want to stop, use the designated parking areas. Visitors are strongly advised not to drive onto the sand as it is very soft, and getting stuck—which can happen only too easily—is a real annoyance. Be cautious, too, about swimming. There are dangerous currents and rip tides, particularly near inlets. The National Park Service recommends swimming only at beaches where lifeguards are on duty.

Bird watchers will delight in the Bodie Island Marshes, near the north entrance to the National Seashore. From various parking areas you may see egrets, herons, glossy ibises and many other species. A bit farther along are the stark bones of the *Laura Barnes*, wrecked in 1921. Keep your eyes open for the remains of other wrecked ships: more than 600 have been recorded. At Pea Island Wildlife Refuge, snow geese by the thousands come to spend the winter months. And way down at the bottom of Hatteras Island is the Cape Hatteras Lighthouse, standing since 1870. It is open to the public; the 198-foot structure with 268 steps is worth climbing for a fantastic view.

Ocracoke, on Ocracoke Island where the National Seashore comes to an end, is a picturesque fishing community much like a New England coastal village. The ship carrying Sir Walter Raleigh's colonists ran aground here on its way to Roanoke Island in 1585, and its passengers were forced to go ashore while repairs were made. In the 1700s, settlers from the mainland used the island for grazing livestock. And a horde of pirates—including the infamous Edward Teach, known as Blackbeard—used Ocracoke Inlet as a refuge from government ships and as a base for their nefarious operations.

There are as many fables told about Teach and his buccaneering career as there were hairs in his bushy black beard, and most of the stories include at least an element of truth. Pirates were supposed to be fierce, but Blackbeard apparently made fierceness almost an art. It is said that he had a habit of braiding his beard and tying the braids with ribbon. A more colorful tale claims that he braided pieces of hemp soaked in lime water or tallow into his beard. Before charging into battle, he would set the hemp afire. Prospective victims would understandably quail before the awful sight of the notorious pirate coming at them like Satan himself, wisps of smoke curling up around his fearsome visage. Still another report says that he would stick long, lighted matches under his hat to create the same effect.

In any case, Blackbeard was obviously a formidable and imaginative foe. He backed up his early version of psychological warfare by arming himself with several daggers, a cutlass and at least six pistols primed, cocked and ready to shoot. His vessel was a captured French merchantman, which he converted into a forty-gun marauder called *Queen Anne's Revenge*.

Blackbeard terrorized the sea-lanes from Virginia to the Caribbean for about two years, from 1716 to 1718. At one point he made an agreement with North Carolina's royal governor, Charles Eden: in return for protection, the pirate would share his ill-gotten prizes. Making Ocracoke Inlet his base, Blackbeard continued to plunder ships at sea and also began to harass landowners along the North Carolina coastline. When not so engaged, he shared a happy home life with his fourteenth wife in the small town of Bath.

The coastal planters soon became fed up with Blackbeard's depredations. Since they could not trust their own governor, they petitioned Alexander Spotswood, lieutenant governor of Virginia, for help. Spotswood dispatched two British sloops under the command of Lt. Robert Maynard. On Nov. 21, 1718, the Naval vessels caught up with Blackbeard in Ocracoke Inlet and engaged him in a bloody battle. Maynard succeeded in killing the pirate in a hand-to-hand struggle. Blackbeard's head was then removed and attached to the end of Maynard's bowsprit; the victorious ship sailed back along the coast to Virginia, triumphantly displaying the horrid token to prove that Blackbeard's reign of terror had truly ended. As with all pirate stories, Blackbeard's includes tempting legends of treasure buried along the Atlantic coast. No trace of it has ever been found, however, and the likelihood is that the old villain spent it all.

Ye Olde Cherokee Inn. A rambling three-story structure with broad porches, Ye Olde Cherokee is right across the road from the Atlantic Ocean, within sight of the Wright Brothers National Memorial in Kill Devil Hills. Built in the 1940s, the building was once a hunting and fishing lodge renowned for its family-style meals, especially the country ham and biscuit breakfasts.

Nowadays, Robert C. and Phyllis Combs operate the Cherokee as a guest house and offer a heap of warm and friendly hospitality. There are seven rooms for travelers: five with one double bed and two with a double and a twin bed. One of the rooms is on the ground floor.

Bed & Breakfast

All accommodations include private baths, heating, air conditioning, carpeting and cable TV.

Continental breakfast is included in the rates. Activities in the area include swimming, sailing, surfing, hang gliding, fishing, bicycling and kite flying.

Ye Olde Cherokee Inn, Rte. 1, Box 315, Kill Devil Hills, NC 27948; (919) 441-6127. (Opposite Wright Brothers Monument on the beach road.) Rates are moderately expensive. American Express, Visa and MasterCard are accepted. Children are welcome; no pets, please. Parking is available. Open year-round.

Beach House. "Beach House" is an appropriate name for this attractive guest house by the sea, but it is really named for its owner, Carol Beach. The house is in Ocracoke, on Silver Lake, Ocracoke's scenic harbor. Built in 1918 as a residence and tourist home by Walter C. O'Neal, a locally renowned hunting and fishing guide, the house remained in the O'Neal family until Ms. Beach purchased it in 1977.

Since then she has been working hard to restore the two-story structure to its original state. It is a durable old place and has withstood many a blow through the years. During a severe storm in 1944, high tides actually entered the house; in order to keep the place from floating off its foundation, Mr. O'Neal cut a "float hole" in the floor of the master bedroom.

Four rooms are available for guests; one bath is shared. All of the rooms are air conditioned. Your hostess offers a continental breakfast, included in the rates, featuring homemade breads and delicious homemade preserves made from Ocracoke-grown figs. All of the village's restaurants and shops are within easy walking distance. Guests are also invited to enjoy the large front porch with a swing and picnic table; the porch overlooks the harbor.

Beach House, Rte. 12, P.O. Box 443, Ocracoke, NC 27960; (919)928-6471. (At the harbor.) Rates are moderate. Children are welcome; no pets, please. Parking is available. Open year-round.

North Carolina

New Bern/Edenton

To reach the southern coast of North Carolina from Ocracoke, take the toll ferry over to Cedar Island, a 2½-hour trip; advance reservations are necessary. Then follow Route 70 to Morehead City. New Bern, the state's first permanent Colonial capital, is a short drive to the northwest. Settled by Germans and Swiss seeking religious and political freedom in the New World, New Bern was named for the city in Switzerland. One of America's most beautiful houses, the Tryon Palace, is located here and is open to the public. The mansion was built in the 1760s for the royal governor, William Tryon, and later became the first state capitol building. In 1798 the structure, except for one wing, was destroyed by fire. For 154 years it lay in ruins. Restoration was begun in 1952, and today the Tryon Palace is an authentic and stunning example of the finest in eighteenth-century architecture.

Northeast of New Bern, on the Albemarle Sound, is the quiet town of Edenton, one of the oldest communities in North Carolina. The area's Crisanti Lake becomes a sanctuary for Canadian geese and other waterfowl from October through March.

Harmony House Inn. Built around 1850, Harmony House has gone through many architectural changes over the years, including being sawed in half to add extra space. It is on the National Register of Historic Places and is designated as a historic point of interest in New Bern. Your hosts, A. E. and Diane Hansen, have preserved the historical flavor through decorating with a combination of antiques and reproductions, many made by local craftsmen. Of particular interest is a picture showing Union soldiers in front of the house during the Civil War. There are nine guest rooms; all have private baths, and three are on the ground floor. Guests are invited to use the parlor; the front porch, which has swings and rocking chairs; and the back yard, which has chairs and a hammock. A complimentary breakfast of coffee cakes, fruit, coffee and juice is served each morning. Historic sites, shops and fine restaurants are all within walking distance of the guest house.

Harmony House Inn, 215 Pollock St., New Bern, NC 28560; (919) 636-3810. Rates are moderately expensive. American Express, Visa and MasterCard are accepted. Children are welcome; no pets, please. Smoking in guest rooms only. Parking available at the house. Open year-round.

Kings Arms. In the heart of New Bern's historic district, the Kings Arms is an exceptionally appealing bed-and-breakfast guest house—elegantly restored and offering a pleasantly homey atmosphere. The house is owned by three couples: Bettye and Walter Paramore, Evelyn and John Peterson, and Uzie and John Thomas. In 1980, they came up with the idea of opening an inn in town for tourists who came to

Bed & Breakfast

see the Tryon Palace and chose this house on Pollock Street for that purpose. The couples named the place Kings Arms after an old New Bern tavern, but it has a good deal of historical significance of its own.

The lot on which the house sits is the back 60 feet of lots three and four on the original plat of New Bern. John Alex Meadows, a carpenter, purchased the 60-by-214-foot lot in 1847 and built the original house. More rooms and the graceful stairway were added around 1898, and in 1905 the size of the house was increased again with the installation of the mansard roof and rooms at the rear. Mrs. Sarah Bradbury bought the place in 1978, renovated it, and converted part of the building into an antique shop. The present owners have restored the stately old home to its past grandeur, and have added bathrooms, facilities for the handicapped and a fire escape.

For guests there are eight double rooms, all with modern private baths, color TV and smoke detectors. Four of the rooms are on the ground floor. The luxurious accommodations, all individually decorated in Colonial style, are furnished with lovely antiques, including canopy, poster and brass beds (with extra-firm mattresses). The rear rooms have two double or queen-size beds; the front rooms offer one double or two twin beds. Rollaway beds for children are available. Each spacious room also includes a handsome fireplace.

Breakfast, included in the rates, consists of juice, coffee or tea and (depending on the day) ham or sausage biscuits, blueberry or English muffins, or toast. Breakfast is served in the small downstairs lobby or brought to your room on a tray. The Tryon Palace is just three blocks away; guided driving tours of the town are available, as are maps and cassettes for walking tours.

Kings Arms, 212 Pollock St., P.O. Box 1085, New Bern, NC 28560; (919) 638-4409. Rates are moderately expensive, lower for longer stays. American Express, Visa and MasterCard are accepted. Children are welcome; no pets, please. Free private parking is available. Open year-round.

North Carolina

The Trestle House Inn. Originally the private home of Joseph S. Crisanti, the Trestle House was opened as an inn in 1983. Its construction is quite unusual: the structure is of California redwood timbers, which were part of a railroad trestle used by the Southern Railway Company. As guests wait for sleep, they can stare up at these massive beams in each room and listen for the nostalgic wail of a distant train crossing the Albemarle Sound trestle.

Your innkeepers, Hal and Louise Worthley, have created a one-of-a-kind retreat. In addition to fishing in a twenty-acre lake (except during October through March, when the lake becomes a bird sanctuary), there are bird-watching blinds, a large game room, billiards, shuffle board, an exercise room, a steam bath and a sun deck For the less athletic, there is a stocked library for your reading enjoyment. There are four guest rooms, two on the ground floor, and all have private baths. Also, the rooms have remote color TV with cable and HBO as well as luxurious beds and linens. Mr. and Mrs. Worthley emphasize "peace, quiet and relaxation." A complimentary continental breakfast is provided. The Trestle House Inn is located just eighty-five miles from the Chesapeake Bay Bridge and Tunnel.

The Trestle House Inn, Route 4, Box 370, Edenton, NC 27932; (919) 482-2282. (From Edenton, take Rte. 32 south 1.8 miles to Airport Road; turn right at the airport sign; 2.8 miles to Trestle House on right.) Rates are moderately expensive. Children over 8 are welcome; no pets, please. Parking at the Inn. Open year-round.

Wilmington

If you continue south along the coast from Morehead City you will come to Wilmington, another historic town, now grown into a city. A 200-block historic district is fun to explore; the British General Cornwallis had his headquarters in the 1771 Burgwin-Wright House, now a museum, and Wilmington's old Cotton Exchange building has been restored to house specialty shops and restaurants. During the Civil War Wilmington was one of the major Confederate ports; more than 200 ships managed to evade the Northern blockade and deliver goods here to be dispersed to the rest of the struggling South.

Children will enjoy a visit to the U.S.S. *North Carolina* Battleship Memorial. Orton Plantation, eighteen miles south of Wilmington overlooking Cape Fear River, offers a year-round display of beautifully landscaped gardens set amidst broad avenues of live oaks. Part of the magnificent ante-bellum mansion dates back to 1730; the house is not open to the public. Airlie Gardens to the east, also part of an old plantation, are particularly lovely in the spring when the azaleas are in bloom.

Anderson Guest House. This delightful bed-and-breakfast establishment in historic downtown Wilmington is owned by Landon and

Bed & Breakfast

Connie Anderson. The main house, of brick and stucco with a fine iron-work piazza and canopy roof, was built by Andrew Jackson Dowling in 1853. In 1890, the structure was significantly enlarged and remodeled in late Victorian style. Double piazzas at the rear of the house face a pretty garden; guests stay in a separate building which also overlooks the garden. There are three air-conditioned double rooms for visitors, each with a private bath. One of the rooms is on the ground floor. Each has a private entrance and working fireplace and is furnished with antiques; one boasts a charming nineteenth-century canopy bed, and magazine pieces from that period pertaining to local history decorate the walls.

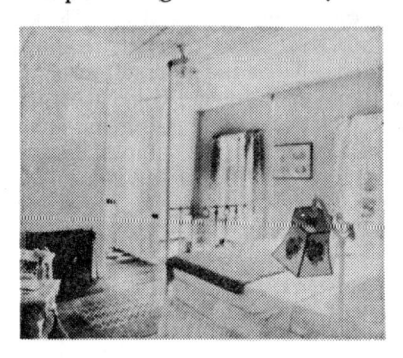

Breakfast, included in the rates, is served during the cooler months in the main house's dining room, which features an unusual vaulted ceiling, cherry woodwork, beautiful stained glass, the original combination gas/electric lighting and a large fireplace. In warmer months guests have their breakfast out in the garden. The menu varies; house specialties include crepes filled with fruits of the season covered with a delicious sauce, and eggs Mornay. In the afternoon, complimentary cocktails are served.

Anderson Guest House, 520 Orange St., Wilmington, NC 28401; (919) 343-8128. Rates are moderately expensive; 1 infant or toddler accommodated free. Children are welcome; no pets, please. Parking is available at the house. Open year-round.

Murchison House. This imposing modified Victorian Gothic, circa 1876, was built by David Reid Murchison and his wife Lucy. The Murchison estate gave the house to the Episcopal Diocese of East Carolina; when that headquarters was moved to another city, Joseph and Lucy Curry purchased the house in 1983. The four guest rooms are large with one or more beds, desks, sofas, chairs, color cable TV, phone, plus reading and writing material. Furnishings are antiques, from 1750 to 1850, as well as fine reproductions. All rooms have private baths. No rooms are on the ground floor. Guests are invited to use the living room and formal dining room. Guests may also relax in the formal garden which has a lovely fountain. Mr. Curry proudly informs guests that his wife fixes a complimentary full country inn breakfast, and "she refuses to serve the same breakfast twice to the same guests!" Visitors are in the center of the town's historic district and only three blocks from shops, restaurants and the famous Cape Fear River Museum.

Murchison House, 305 S. Third St., Wilmington, NC 28401; (919) 343-8580. Rates are moderately expensive, with discounts for longer stays. American Express, Visa and MasterCard are accepted. Children are welcome; no pets, please. Parking available at the house. Open year-round.

The Piedmont (Midlands) Region
Raleigh/Greensboro/Winston-Salem

Raleigh, North Carolina's capital, was laid out in 1792 and named for that courtly soldier, explorer and colonizer, Sir Walter Raleigh. The colony's legislators, according to local tales, chose the site because it was only four miles from a popular tavern. Running a government can be a trying, throat-drying occupation, and the need for a soothing dram was once again catered to after the Civil War, during the Reconstruction period. A rowdy group of carpetbagger politicians set up their own bar in the old Capitol Building, which still has nicks in its steps from the whiskey barrels rolled up to quench their thirst.

North Carolina's dynamic mix of industry, particularly tobacco,

Bed & Breakfast

textiles and furniture, is most evident in the central Piedmont region. Durham and Winston-Salem are both large tobacco centers. Durham, northwest of Raleigh, is also the home of Duke University. The University of North Carolina, founded in 1795 and the oldest state university in the United States, is in Chapel Hill, just beyond Durham. Greensboro, a few miles farther north, is the home town of O. Henry (William Sydney Porter), the famed American author of short stories.

In Winston-Salem to the west, Old Salem, an eighteenth-century Moravian community, provides a fascinating glimpse into an unusual way of life. The Moravians emigrated from Germany in 1735 and set up their first community in America in Savannah, Georgia. Six years later they moved to Pennsylvania; in 1766, a group moved back to the South to found Salem. (Salem merged with the neighboring town of Winston in 1913.) More than thirty of the Moravians' original structures have been restored. Early crafts are demonstrated in the Single Brothers House, built in 1769, and at Christmastime visitors are invited to sample traditional Moravian sugar buns and lebkuchen, holiday cookies made with honey, almonds and orange peel. While you nibble, you can watch beeswax candles being dipped for the Christmas Eve Love Feast services.

The Oakwood Inn. Located in Raleigh's historic district and within walking distance of the Capitol area, the Oakwood is operated by Chris Yetter and Oakley L. Herring. The Italianate home, circa 1871, was built by Kenneth C. Raynor and is listed on the National Register

North Carolina

of Historic Places. Period antique furnishings and accessories give individual character to each of the six guest rooms, two of which are on the ground floor. The ground-floor rooms have private baths, and the other four rooms share two baths. A complimentary, full-course breakfast is served, including fresh fruit, a main course, side dishes and hot breads. Guests are invited to use the parlor for friendly conversation. Lovers of period architecture can wander the twenty square blocks of 1870-to-1920 homes in the historic district and admire the gardens, stained-glass windows, steep gables and intricate gingerbread details that reflect the bygone Victorian era. Other activities can be coordinated through the Capitol Area Visitor's Center, which is also near the Oakwood Inn.

The Oakwood Inn, 411 N. Bloodworth St., Raleigh, NC 27604; (919) 832-9712. Rates range from moderately expensive to expensive, with special discounts for longer stays. American Express, Visa and MasterCard are accepted. Children over 12 are welcome; no pets, please. There are 10 parking places available. Open year-round.

Greenwood. Just three minutes from downtown Greensboro is the eighty-year-old, chalet-style Greenwood. Jo Anne and Lee Green invite you to relax in their five guest rooms, eclectically decorated

with artwork from their travels. One guest room is on the ground floor and has a private bath. One other room has a private bath, and three rooms share a bath. Guests may use the living room, TV lounge, guest kitchen and snack room. Visitors will also enjoy the Green's collection of wood carvings. Included in the rates is a delicious breakfast of fresh fruit and juices; homemade breads and muffins; cold cereal; coffee, tea and milk. In the afternoon, there is complimentary wine, cheese and tea. Visitors will enjoy the Greensboro

Bed & Breakfast

Historical Museum, Guilford Battleground, Water Country USA and numerous outlet malls.

Greenwood, 205 N. Park Dr., P.O. Box 6948, Greensboro, NC 27415; (919) 656-7908. (Seven blocks north of downtown between Elm and Church streets and south of Wendover Avenue.) Rates range from moderate to moderately expensive; weekly and monthly rates available. No charge for babies; $10 extra for small children. American Express, Visa and MasterCard are accepted. Children are welcome; no pets, please. Parking available across the street. Open year-round.

The Greenwich Inn. Historic "Old Greensborough" is the site of the Greenwich Inn, managed by Alexy P. Richy. The building, constructed in 1898, was the office of Cone Mills and later became a residential hotel. Restoration in 1982 created a small inn with a definite European style. Twenty-eight rooms are elegantly furnished in eighteenth-century antiques. Special complimentary amenities include valet parking; imported wine and cheese served in the room each evening; turn-down bed service with a chocolate mint on the pillow; and a continental breakfast consisting of croissant, sugar cake, coffee and orange juice delivered on a silver platter to the room with the morning paper. A cozy lobby area is a favorite place for guests to relax, and some prefer eating their breakfast there. Downtown Greensboro offers shopping, dining and dancing.

The Greenwich Inn, 111 Washington St., Greensboro, NC 27401; (919) 272-3474. (Write for a detailed map and brochure.) Rates are moderately expensive with special rates for longer stays. Children 18 and younger stay free of charge. American Express, Visa and MasterCard are accepted. No pets, please. Open year-round.

Brookstown Inn Bed & Breakfast. Within the walls of an 1830s cotton mill in Winston-Salem, you will find a forty-room bed-and-breakfast inn that combines the romance vacationers enjoy with the convenience business people need. Rooms are decorated with Appalachian handmade quilts, custom-made armoires, seventeenth- and eighteenth-century primitive antiques as well as twentieth-century "industrial chic" concepts. Twelve rooms are on the ground floor, and all rooms have private baths as well as remote-control cable TV and private telephones. Some rooms have fireplaces and others have whirlpool baths. Included in the rates is a breakfast that reflects the influence of the Moravians who settled in Old Salem. Guests will enjoy the homebaked Moravian sugar cake and Love Feast buns, coffee and freshly squeezed citrus juice. Breakfast is served in the dining room on elegant china and linen. An Irish cupboard, which displays a collection of antique pewter, porcelains and teapots, adds charm to the dining area. The antique-filled parlor is open for guests to relax and chat over wine and a bit of brie from 5 until 7 p.m. There is also a modern spa bath to enjoy. The Inn is in the historic

North Carolina

Brookstown Mill complex, which features elegant specialty shops and restaurants and is also convenient to downtown businesses and other attractions.

Brookstown Inn Bed & Breakfast, 200 Brookstown Ave., Winston-Salem, NC 27101; (919) 725-1120. (Just 2 blocks off I-40.) Rates range from moderately expensive to expensive. American Express, Visa and MasterCard are accepted. Children are welcome; no pets, please. Parking provided adjacent to the Inn. Open year-round.

Colonel Ludlow House. If only one word were used to describe the Col. Ludlow House it would be "enchanting." Everywhere you turn, there is a new architectural or decorating surprise. The house was built in 1887 and is one of the best examples of Queen Anne architecture in the area. There's hand-wrought stenciling on the front screen door; each room has original stained-glass windows; the dining room is papered with an 1888 dresser reproduction wall covering; guests sleep under hand-crocheted bedspreads of tobacco twine plus eyelet sheets and pillow cases; and even the flowers on the front steps were selected to complement the Victorian house. The proprietor, H. Kenneth Land, got the idea for opening a guest house when he stayed in the Eliza Thompson House in Savannah. Although he was formerly a high school English teacher, Mr. Land has been restoring old houses full-time since 1972. His manager for the Ludlow House is Carol Royals.

There are fifteen rooms, three on the ground floor. All rooms have private baths (and some have a two-person whirlpool tub). Lots of little extras make this house special: a tiny reading light on the

Bed & Breakfast

headboard; a small alarm clock and a telephone by the bed; an individual stereo system with an assortment of tapes; fresh flowers; a tiny refrigerator; a coffeemaker; classic books; and a complimentary bottle of wine.

The complimentary breakfast can be served in your room, but then (weather permitting) you would miss dining on the wonderful wicker-furnished front porch or in the formal dining room, which has oak- and cane-bottomed chairs and a definite Victorian warmth. Whatever location you choose, breakfast is a treat of coffee, tea, fresh orange juice, fresh fruit cup and assorted fancy pastries—all served on fine china, crystal and silver. Gourmet restaurants, cafes, shops and parks are all within walking distance. Also, guests are within three blocks of the YMCA and YWCA. Bicycles are provided by your hosts.

Colonel Ludlow House, Summit and West 5th, Winston-Salem, NC 27101; (919) 777-1887. Rates are expensive. American Express, Visa and MasterCard are accepted. Children over 10 are welcome; no pets, please. Parking available at the house. Open year-round.

Pinehurst

In the southern Piedmont region two year-round resorts, Southern Pines and Pinehurst, have become world famous for both equestrian sports and superb golf. Southern Pines is the home of North Carolina's oldest organized hunt, and during the winter months the members regularly ride out on fox and drag hunts. In early April, Southern Pines hosts the Stoneybrook Steeplechase Races.

Pinehurst offers the World Golf Hall of Fame, on Gerald R. Ford Boulevard, with displays portraying the history of golf along with photographs of famous golfers and other memorabilia. The Colgate Hall of Fame Golf Classic is held at the Pinehurst Country Club every August. If neither horses nor whacking away at a small white ball appeals to you, excellent tennis and hunting, and many elegant shops, are also nearby.

Pinehurst is not actually a town, but a privately owned corporation. Founded in 1845, it was the brainchild of James Walker Tufts, a Boston philanthropist. His idea was to create a retreat for fellow Northerners who might wish to escape the snow and ice of winter. Tufts asked Frederick Law Olmsted, the renowned landscape architect, to design the place. Olmsted created a charming village that combines the lush greenery and flowers of the South with the traditional ambiance of New England; there is even a village green. And to make your stay in Pinehurst even more pleasurable, the village includes a delightful bed-and-breakfast guest house, the Magnolia Inn.

The Magnolia Inn. Situated right in the center of Pinehurst, the Magnolia Inn is a beautiful, spacious old house. Two broad porches,

North Carolina

one on the ground level and another which runs all the way around the second floor, are comfortable places to sit and relax. Built in 1896 by the Tufts family, founders of Pinehurst, the white-painted structure has always been used as a guest house. The present owner, Leslie Wilson, purchased it in 1967 and runs it with the help of her two daughters.

Accommodations include one single, nine double, and three triple rooms for guests; all have private baths, twin beds and air conditioning. Two of the rooms are on the ground floor, as is a pleasant living room with color TV and card tables. There is a swimming pool on the lovely tree-shaded grounds for summer use, and in wintertime guests are invited to enjoy a crackling fire in the living room.

A full breakfast is included in the very reasonable rates; the house specialty is blueberry pancakes made with native North Carolina berries. Several excellent restaurants and an array of fine shops are within walking distance. Horseback riding and tennis are available nearby, and as a guest at Magnolia Inn you are welcome to play golf at Pinehurst Country Club on any of its six magnificent eighteen-hole courses.

The Magnolia Inn, Magnolia Road, P.O. Box 266, Pinehurst, NC 28374; (919)295-6900. Rates are moderate. No charge except for breakfast for children under 16. Children are welcome; no pets, please. Parking is available. Open year-round.

Charlotte

The largest city in the Carolinas and the center of North Carolina's

Bed & Breakfast

textile industry, Charlotte was founded in 1748. The region was, until the 1848 California Gold Rush, the country's largest producer of gold. A U.S. Mint was operated here from 1837 to 1913; the building now exhibits American and European paintings, sculpture and decorative arts. Spirit Square Arts Center, formerly a Byzantine-style church, offers regular musical and theatrical performances. For children (of all ages) there is Carowinds, an amusement park with a large selection of rides, and Ocean Island, a swimming pool with manmade waves. The park is ten miles south of Charlotte on the North Carolina/South Carolina border.

The Blair-Bowden House. John M. Bowden welcomes guests to his attractive bed-and-breakfast guest house in Charlotte's historic Fourth Ward. The old frame house, with a railed front porch, was built in 1907—possibly by Lewis Asbury, Charlotte's first native son architect. Originally constructed as a country home, the house was owned by the Blair family. The entrance room, according to your host, is "the ultimate corruption of the medieval Great Room"; the Blair daughters called it "a courting parlor." Many of the Victorian elements were removed during a 1922 renovation, but the present owner has restored some of them.

For guests there are two rooms with fireplaces and a suite with a sitting room, wet bar, whirlpool and three fireplaces. All are luxuriously furnished with nineteenth-century American and English pieces, and all have private baths. Continental breakfast, which is included in the rates, features your host's own homemade Moravian sugar cake, coffee or tea, and—in season—fruits. Other meals may be served, at extra charge, by arrangement. The Blair-Bowden House, in the heart of uptown Charlotte, is a short walk from restaurants, shops and other attractions including Spirit Square Arts Center and Discovery Place Science Museum.

The Blair-Bowden House, 529 N. Poplar St., Charlotte, NC 28202; (704)334-

8909. (Corner of North Poplar and West 9th Street.) Rates are moderately expensive for rooms and expensive for the suite. Children are welcome on a limited basis; no pets, please. On-street parking in front of the house is available. Open year-round.

Hampton Manor. Mr. and Mrs. B. M. Triggs invite you to sample palatial luxury "in the European tradition of accommodating guests elegantly." Built in the style of the 1840s English manor house "Rosehill," this manor house is filled with antiques and has an Empire-style formal dining room and an informal English pub-style parlor. (There are ultra-modern conveniences to enjoy: a hot tub Jacuzzi; a Rolls Royce Silver Shadow for trips to the airport and other travel requirements; individual wet bars and kitchenettes.) Four private bedroom suites are available, two on the ground floor, and all with private baths. Continental or full English breakfast, included in the rates, is served in the privacy of each suite. Guests are also invited to partake of English tea in the afternoon, and they may use the English pub, meeting rooms and offices. In addition, Hampton Manor has an olympic-size swimming pool, lawn croquet and tennis courts.

Hampton Manor, 3327 Carmel Road, Charlotte, NC 28211; (704) 542-6299. Rates are expensive ($150–$300 per night). American Express, Visa and MasterCard are available. Children and pets are welcome. Valet parking on site. Open year-round.

The Homeplace. Peggy and Frank Dearien have designed the Homeplace brochure to read like a personal invitation to their guests. "At The Homeplace, the warm and friendly atmosphere hasn't changed a bit since 1902. (Completely restored in 1983.) The moment you drive up to this country Victorian bed and breakfast home, leave

Bed & Breakfast

your cares behind you and prepare to visit the past." The past comes alive on the wraparound porch with country rockers; the tin roof makes rain showers a joy; fireplaces and heart-of-pine floors adorn every room; a country motif is carried throughout the house with quilts, antiques, primitive paintings (done by Mrs. Dearien's father who began painting at age 79); and the original hand-crafted staircase and 10-foot beaded ceilings. The downstairs Victorian-style bedroom has a private entrance and bath. The two upstairs bedrooms share a large semi-private bath.

An inviting, complimentary breakfast treats guests to homemade biscuits, jams, muffins, date-nut bread with cream cheese, coffee cake or pastry. Fresh fruit may include a baked apple or broiled grapefruit. (Mr. and Mrs. Dearien both cook your entire fare.) Weekends offer an egg casserole or sausage biscuits—your hosts call it "deluxe continental." Guests are invited to use the parlor, watch TV, read or simply visit and indulge in the various appetizers or desserts prepared by Peggy and Frank. Guests are only ten minutes from major shopping centers, downtown, art and science museums, and the Coliseum. Day trips include furniture and textile outlets as well as antique shops.

The Homeplace, 5901 Sardis Rd., Charlotte, NC 28226; (704) 365-1936. Rates are moderately expensive. Visa and MasterCard are accepted. A 10% discount is given for stays over four nights. Children over 10 are welcome; no pets, please. Your hosts ask that smoking be done on the porches only. Ample parking available. Open year-round.

North Carolina's Mountains

The western portion of the state is one of extravagant beauty—of ancient, blue-hazed mountains and deep valleys, spectacular water-

North Carolina

falls and white-water gorges, quaint mountain towns and an ever-changing display of flowers and foliage. The most enjoyable way to explore the region is to follow the North Carolina section of the Blue Ridge Parkway. The scenic highway, which starts in Virginia's Shenandoah National Forest to the north and ends at Cherokee, North Carolina, is open year-round except for temporary shut-downs due to winter snow or ice or occasional summer fog. Numerous overlooks offer splendid views, and there are hiking trails galore. A few old highland farms may still be seen, with their weathered barns and split-rail fences, and in the towns adjacent to the parkway the descendants of long-ago settlers still practice many of the old-time customs.

Along the way, sharp-eyed travelers may also spot some of the region's abundance of wildlife—chipmunks, skunks, foxes and raccoons. White-tailed deer usually stay deep within the forest, but may sometimes be observed near the road at dawn or dusk. Bears, too, may appear at these times, but they are unpredictable. Do not try to feed a bear, even if it does look amiable. Bears do not know the difference between a sandwich and your arm. If you stop for a picnic beside a mountain stream or take a hike along a trail, be sure to tightly close your car's doors and windows. Bears are clever creatures, quite capable of climbing in after your food supply. It can be a nasty shock to return to your vehicle and find it occupied by a very large, furry beast. A surprised bear will usually run away. (So will a surprised human.) But with bears, one never knows for sure.

The towns of Boone, Blowing Rock, Banner Elk and Linville are located at the northern end of North Carolina's Blue Ridge Parkway. All popular summer vacation resorts, they also offer excellent winter skiing facilities. Scattered throughout the region are a host of shops displaying locally handcrafted items including strip-oak baskets, cornshuck dolls, fireplace brooms, wooden toys and musical instruments, quilts, rustic furniture and hand-turned pottery.

Boone

The town of Boone is named for Daniel Boone, who lived in a cabin here in the 1760s. One mile east of town, the Daniel Boone Native Gardens offers an extensive collection of native plants and flowers in a natural setting. If you're in the area in summertime, attend a performance of *Horn in the West*, an exciting drama held in an outdoor amphitheater on the same grounds as the gardens. Back in 1776, when the Blue Ridge Mountains marked the frontier, American colonists "heard a horn blowing in the West." The "horn" called them to battle with the British forces and their fierce Indian allies. The story relates that from deep in the mountains of western North Carolina the people responded, including a group led by Daniel Boone. The mountaineers surrounded and engaged the British troops, defeating them soundly.

Bed & Breakfast

Ole Waterloo. Octogenarian Thelma Jennie Greene has a delightful story of how her guest house got its unusual name. It seems that a creek runs under the house and used to flood the place from time to time. Before Mrs. Greene bought the place in 1965 and installed drain pipes for the water to run through, the house had defeated every owner —like Napoleon at *his* Waterloo.

Today the house is dry and cozy, an attractive stone-sided structure set amid mountain firs. Your hostess has six guest rooms, including accommodations for singles, doubles and triples; three of the rooms are on the ground floor. There are one private and two semi-private baths. In addition, a cottage on the grounds accommodates five people. Guests are invited to enjoy Mrs. Greene's living room and wide front porch, and breakfast will be provided if requested, for an extra charge. Visitors may also use the kitchen for other meals.

Ole Waterloo was built in 1910, and therefore is old enough to have a resident ghost. Although Mrs. Greene was told by previous owners that a ghost walked the house at night, she has never seen it. If you have an affinity with the spirit world, you might be lucky enough to meet the walker. If not, just ignore the whole thing.

Ole Waterloo, P.O. Box 30, Boone, NC 28607; (704) 264-8034. (One mile west of Boone Police Station on Rte. 421.) Rates are moderate, lower for longer stays. Children and pets are welcome. Parking is available. Open year-round.

Blowing Rock

From Boone, take Route 321 south a few miles to Blowing Rock. Along the way, stop for a ride on the Tweetsie Railroad. The chuffing, tooting, authentic old coal-fired locomotive pulls open-air coaches on a three-mile trip during which the train is "attacked" by Indians and train robbers. You might also enjoy a stop at Mystery Hill nearby, where water runs uphill and people standing in the Mystery House seem to be leaning at an impossible angle. It's hokey, but fun. The adjacent Antique Museum includes a fascinating clutter of items used in the old days in these mountains.

A resort for more than eighty years, the town of Blowing Rock was named for a nearby cliff that overhangs Johns River Gorge 3000 feet below. Any light object, such as a handkerchief, that is thrown over the edge of the rock will float right back up. A romantic Indian legend about the phenomenon relates the tale of a young Cherokee brave who leaped from the rock to return to his tribe in the wilderness far below. His sweetheart, the daughter of a Chickasaw chieftain, was grief-stricken, believing that her lover had died in the fall. Nevertheless, she prayed daily to the Great Spirit, asking for her hero's return. Then, the legend continues, on an evening with a reddening sky, a sudden gust of wind blew the young man back onto the rock and into her arms. And from that day, a perpetual wind has blown up onto

North Carolina

the rock from the valley below. The stark scientific explanation is that the rocky walls of the gorge form a flume through which the northwest wind sweeps with such force that it returns objects cast out over the void.

Maple Lodge. An exceptionally inviting guest house, Maple Lodge is owned by Jack and Rheba Crane. The attractive lodge, built in 1946, is surrounded by trees, shrubbery and a nice lawn with comfortable wicker chairs. The decor is, according to Mrs. Crane, turn-of-the-century "Grandmother's House"; your hosts continually search out and add pieces of old oak furniture and other treasures. One of their more recent acquisitions is an old pump organ.

For guests there are eight rooms in the main house, each with a private bath, and a two-bedroom cottage with two baths. Guests are welcome to use the two parlors and large "Florida" room in the lodge; on chilly evenings the stone fireplace in the small parlor offers a

cheery blaze. A continental breakfast of juice, fruit, muffins or breakfast breads and coffee or milk is included in the rates.

Maple Lodge is just off Main Street and within walking distance of restaurants, shops and churches. The Blue Ridge Parkway is a mile away, and the Cranes will gladly suggest things to do in the area, such as horseback riding, hiking and shopping for handcrafted gifts

It seems appropriate here to quote a local resident, ninety-year-old Mrs. Mary Beck, concerning the community of Blowing Rock and Maple Lodge. She says: "We old-time residents have until recently kept to 'the mountain atmosphere,' but our influx of newcomers is

Bed & Breakfast

trying to make the place 'citified.' People come here because they like the quiet atmosphere and think it would be a nice place to live—then, after they get here they try to make it like the place they come from!" Maple Lodge, she notes, is special. "It's truly a lovely place, and Blowing Rock never had anything so elegant. I can heartily recommend it and feel that anyone who stays in this charming house will be delighted."

Maple Lodge, P.O. Box 66, Sunset Drive, Blowing Rock, NC 28605; (704) 295-3331. (Next to Blowing Rock Elementary School.) Rates are expensive. Children are welcome; no pets, please. Parking is available. Open May 1–October.

From Blowing Rock, follow Route 221 to Linville and Grandfather Mountain. This ancient peak is 5964 feet high, with a steep, winding road leading to the summit. Along the way are rock formations said to be a billion years old, and up on top you can cross a scary but safe swinging bridge for a marvelous 360-degree view of the region. Linville Gorge and its spectacular falls are a few miles to the south. The Linville River, one of the state's wildest white-water streams, originates high on the slopes of Grandfather Mountain and drops more than 2000 feet through the gorge's twelve-mile stretch of deep, curving canyon. Linville Caverns, another notable sight, is on Route 221 between Linville and Marion.

Asheville/Hendersonville/Lake Lure/Tryon

Back on the Blue Ridge Parkway again, you will come to the turnoff (Route 128) for Mt. Mitchell State Park. An auto road leads to the summit of the 6684-foot mountain. Farther along the parkway will be the turnoff for Asheville, where visitors may explore the Thomas Wolfe Memorial at 40 Spruce St. The renowned novelist grew up in Asheville and lived in this rambling Victorian home, which his mother ran as a boarding house.

The absolute opposite of a simple rooming house is the Biltmore Mansion, two miles south of Asheville on Route 25, off Interstate 40. The magnificent 250-room French Renaissance chateau, designed by Richard Morris Hunt for George W. Vanderbilt, is situated on an 11,000-acre estate with 35 acres of formal gardens laid out by Frederick Law Olmsted. More than 500 varieties of azaleas are grown here, and the 4-acre English walled garden is said to be the finest in America.

A number of the mansion's most interesting and best-furnished rooms are open to visitors; house and gardens are open year-round except Thanksgiving, Christmas and New Year's Day. Completed in 1896, the chateau contains an almost endless list of treasures: Napoleon's chess set; prints by Durer and Landseer; Portuguese, Spanish and Italian eighteenth- and nineteenth-century furnishings; portraits by Sargent and Whistler, and much, much more. The 72- by

North Carolina

42-foot banquet hall, arching 75 feet high, is graced with two late nineteenth-century Gothic thrones and five rare sixteenth-century Flemish tapestries. The library, with more than 20,000 volumes, has a strikingly beautiful painted ceiling attributed to Pellegrini; one bedroom is paneled in walnut, and another's walls are covered with yellow silk.

During the summer months Asheville presents a series of country dance and music concerts, including Shindig-on-the-Green and the Mountain Dance and Folk Festival. Brevard, to the south, offers the Summer Festival of Music with symphonic, choral, chamber and operatic performances. Over in Flat Rock, about thirty miles southwest of Asheville near Hendersonville, you can visit Carl Sandburg's home and farm where the famed poet, writer and historian lived for more than two decades. In the same area, the North Carolina State Theater's Flat Rock Playhouse presents a series of dramas from late June through August. Tryon, with a gentle climate year-round, boasts long springs and autumns, horse shows and fox hunts, and excellent golf, tennis, fishing and swimming.

Flint Street Inn. Rick and Lynne Vogel invite you to enjoy their turn-of-the-century inn, which is in the Montford Historic District and within easy walking distance of Asheville's business district. Built in 1915 as a family home, the Flint Street Inn has been lovingly renovated to reflect the style and tradition that constitute Southern hospitality. In fact, the Vogels say their Inn will probably remind guests of their grandmother's house; treasures from that bygone era are scattered about. There are four upper-floor guest rooms, two with private baths. A rocking chair–laden front porch overlooks a lush yard filled with trees and rhododendron, and a pleasant parlor and

Bed & Breakfast

dining room are for guests' enjoyment. Included in the rates is a full Southern-style breakfast of orange juice; coffee, tea or milk; homemade biscuits, muffins or toast; choice of eggs; sausage or bacon; assorted jellies and the morning paper! Guests may unwind in the evening over a complimentary glass of wine, and they may take advantage of the Vogels' other business, Asheville Outings—a touring company which includes day trips to Biltmore Village, the Blue Ridge Parkway area and Carl Sandburg's home, to mention only a few.

Flint Street Inn, 116 Flint St., Asheville, NC 28801; (704) 253-6723. (Easily accessible by keeping the Civic Center on your right going north on Haywood Street. Passing over I-240, Haywood Street becomes Flint Street. The Inn is 4 houses beyond the corner of Flint Street and Starnes Avenue, on the left.) Rates are moderately expensive; discount for longer stays. American Express, Visa and MasterCard are accepted. Children over 12 are welcome; no pets, please. Lighted, off-street parking available. Open year-round.

The Ray House Bed and Breakfast. If the walls of Ray House could only talk! Natives tell of how F. Scott Fitzgerald was a visitor to the house during the time he and Zelda lived in Asheville. In fact, he bought a touring car from the family who owned the house at the time. Also, there was Lamar Stringfield, conductor of the North Carolina Symphony and winner of a Pulitzer Prize in 1928 for his composition *From the Southern Mountains*, the fourth movement of which is the theme "Cripple Creek." Mr. Stringfield was a nephew of the Ray family. Your hosts are as interesting as the legends that go with the house. Alice Curtis is a former French teacher whose interests include languages, art and music. Will Curtis is an editorial writer for the *Asheville Times* and is interested in gardening, geology and outdoor activities. Both love cooking, travel, old houses and antiques—which is evident in the bed and breakfast they operate. The style of the house is Colonial revival/craftsman; it was built in 1891 by Capt. John Edwin Ray who was involved in the development of Asheville. Dark beams and woodwork against white walls and

North Carolina

wallpaper give it the feeling of an English country home. Antiques and "collectibles" decorate the house, including a collection of antique culinary equipment in the kitchen. Three guest rooms are available, none on the ground floor. There is one private bath and another shared bath, which is decided by occupancy. Included in the rates is a continental breakfast, served in the formal dining room, which consists of orange juice, coffee or tea, homemade jams and jellies, and sweet breads. Lemon Loaf is a house specialty. Guests may choose to have breakfast on the wraparound porch which overlooks the almost parklike setting created by lush trees, shrubs and flowers. A view of downtown Asheville and the surrounding neighborhood makes the porch a favorite place to relax. Guests are also encouraged to use the library, where there is a collection of books on Asheville; the music room, which has an antique grand piano; or relax in the beamed living room. Nearby is the University of North Carolina at Asheville and its lovely Botanical Gardens.

The Ray House Bed and Breakfast, 83 Hillside St., Asheville, NC 28801; (704) 252-0106. Rates are moderate with special rates for longer stays. Children are welcome; no pets, please. Parking available at the house. Open year-round.

The Old Reynolds Mansion. When Fred and Helen Faber first saw this deteriorated ante-bellum mansion, their restoration experience convinced them that it was salvageable, despite the fact that one person recommended bulldozing it instead. After they purchased the house, it took them two years to get the bed and breakfast ready for occupants. Guests are now invited to sample the ten guest rooms, each decorated in a different style, from Early American to Oriental. A Bridal Suite features an 1890 brass bed and claw-footed tub in the room near the fireplace. As with many old houses, there seems to

Bed & Breakfast

be a resident ghost. Footsteps are heard in one room on the third floor, the lights go off and the door swings open. Other than that, it seems to be friendly enough. Three of the guest rooms have private baths, and the other seven rooms share three baths. No rooms are available on the ground floor. A complimentary breakfast of coffee, tea or hot chocolate; fresh fruit in season; orange juice; and homebaked muffins, nut breads, and coffee cake is served in the formal dining room. For enjoyment, the Fabers have a front parlor which has a wood-burning fireplace and reading materials or games. The second floor has a seating area for guest use. There is also a refrigerator and an ice maker for visitors. Encourage the Fabers to share their stories about the restoration—their sense of humor during adversity is amazing! Trout fishing, white-water rafting and various tours are available; if weather permits, guests enjoy a swimming pool on the grounds.

The Old Reynolds Mansion, 100 Reynolds Heights, Asheville, NC 28804; (704) 254-0496. (Take Merrimon Avenue, Rte. 25 North past Beaver Lake. Turn right just past stop light onto Beaver Street. Turn left up gravel lane.) Rates are moderate; discount for longer stays. Well-behaved children are welcome; no pets, please. Private parking at the house. Open year-round.

Reverie Bed and Breakfast. Right in the heart of the Blue Ridge Mountains in Reverie, Kathy and Michael Abriola offer a friendly travel alternative. The Colonial Revival–style house, built in 1911, has always been either a boarding or guest house. But the Abriolas have added a romantic ambiance created by the Victorian surroundings mixed with the subtle "decadence" of Art Deco. There are eight guest rooms, three with private baths and two sharing a bath. One guest room is on the ground floor and has a private bath. Each room has a sink with hot and cold water. The Abriolas have refreshments to welcome guests upon arrival, and also included in the rates is a continental breakfast of fresh-ground coffee, fresh-squeezed orange juice or local apple juice, croissants, fresh-baked muffins, fruit and the morning paper. North Carolina's State Theatre, The Flat Rock Playhouse, and the Carl Sandburg home are approximately one mile away. This area of the state is especially glorious at the height of autumn colors.

Reverie Bed and Breakfast, 1197 Greenville Highway, Hendersonville, NC 28739; (704) 693-8255. (Take I-26 to Exit 18; US-64 west into Hendersonville; turn left on US-25.) Rates are moderately expensive; discounts for longer stays and senior citizens. American Express, Visa and MasterCard are accepted. Children 12 and over are welcome; no pets or smoking, please. Parking available on the grounds. Open March 15–Nov. 15.

The Lodge on Lake Lure. Originally built as a refuge for the N.C. Highway Patrol back in the early 1930s, the lodge has been transformed into a vacation retreat by Allen and Doris Nunn. The Lodge

North Carolina

is the only non-residential property located directly on Lake Lure, and the Nunns have worked hard to preserve the traditional mountain feeling and the idyllic charm found in the town of Lake Lure. There are eleven guest rooms, five on the ground floor. Family suites are available, and all rooms have private baths. Guests are free to use the game room, which has a TV; the lodge's great room, which features a giant stone fireplace and overstuffed chairs; or the porch, which is a wonderful place to rock and take in the glorious mountain views. In addition, the lodge has a private boathouse where guests may rent a water-ski rig, canoes or jon boats. There are twenty-seven miles of shoreline, and quiet coves provide excellent fishing. An easy walk from the lodge is a nine-hole municipal golf course. A complimentary continental breakfast of fresh breads, fruits, juices, preserves, coffee, tea and milk is provided. For a nominal fee, a more hearty mountain breakfast is available as are picnic box lunches. Beverage service is also extra. The town of Lake Lure is a short drive away. Travelers are ninety miles west of Charlotte, twenty-five miles east of Asheville, and just eighteen miles from Interstate 26.

The Lodge on Lake Lure, Rte. 1, Box 529 A, Lake Lure, NC 28746; (704) 625-2789. (The lodge is on Charlotte Drive, just off US-64/74. Write for a map/brochure.) Rates range from moderately expensive to expensive. Special rates available for longer stays. American Express, Visa and MasterCard are accepted. Due to the proximity of very deep water, only well-behaved and constantly supervised children are invited. No pets, please. Parking available at the lodge. Open year-round.

Mill Farm Inn. Just outside of Tryon, the charming Mill Farm Inn offers bed and breakfast and a friendly, homelike atmosphere. A handsome native-stone house, Mill Farm was built in 1939 on the site of an old gristmill that was destroyed by fire. The building served as an inn until the early 1950s, then was a private residence for twenty years. Chip and Penny Kessler purchased Mill Farm in 1980 and opened it once again for guests in 1982.

Eight spacious twin-bedded rooms are available for travelers,

Bed & Breakfast

including several one- or two-bedroom suites, all with private baths. Two of the rooms are on the ground floor. There's also a large living room with a fireplace, and sitting porches offer shady outdoor spots for relaxing. All of the indoor areas are air conditioned and are furnished in traditional style with fine period reproductions.

Breakfast, included in the rates and served in the attractive dining room, offers juice, English muffins and a daily special bread (banana, oatmeal applesauce, brown breakfast bread, etc.), preserves and jelly, coffee, tea or milk. Guests may also use the inn's kitchen if they wish. Mill Farm is situated in historic Pacolet River Valley on the southern slopes of the Blue Ridge Mountains. The river flows past the rear boundary of the Kesslers' 3½ acres, which abound with flowers and greenery. Bird watching is highly recommended.

Your hosts are also the proprietors of another excellent establishment, L'Auberge of Tryon. L'Auberge, a modern structure in downtown Tryon, offers one- and two-bedroom suites and studios for a week or longer stays. The accommodations include modern kitchens and baths, new furnishings and decorations, air conditioning, fireplaces, patio-deck and garden.

Mill Farm Inn, P.O. Box 1251, Tryon, NC 28782; (704)859-6992. (Mill Farm Inn is on Rte. 108, 2½ miles from I-26 and 1½ miles from downtown Tryon.) Rates are moderately expensive, lower for children. Children are welcome, if attended; no pets, please. Parking is available. Open March 1–Dec. 1. (Special arrangements can be made for time between Dec. 1 and March 1 for parties of 6 or more.)

Cherokee/Bryson City/Franklin/Glenville

The Blue Ridge Parkway comes to an end at Cherokee. The descendants of the Cherokee people who escaped being forcibly marched to Oklahoma over the tragic "Trail of Tears" in the mid-1800s still live here on their own reservation, on Route 441 just north of the town. To see how the Cherokees lived 200 years ago, explore the Oconaluftee Indian Village, open to visitors from mid-May to late October. You can watch Indians in traditional tribal dress making log canoes, weaving baskets or creating exquisite beadwork. The Museum of the Cherokee Indians (open all year) houses arts, crafts, audio-visual displays and prehistoric artifacts. And the moving drama *Unto These Hills,* relating the history of the Cherokee Nation from 1540 to 1838, is presented on summer evenings at Mountainside Theatre, a natural amphitheater next to the Indian Village.

From Cherokee, Route 441 leads through the Great Smoky Mountains National Park to Gatlinburg, Tennessee, and beyond. Route 19 out of Cherokee heads west to Bryson City. Off of Route 19 between the two towns, Route 28 South goes to Franklin; Glenville is a scenic drive south and east. Each of these old mountain towns has a bed and breakfast, and any one of them would make an excellent base from which to explore the region.

Folkestone Lodge. Outdoor sports enthusiasts will love Folkestone Lodge! Located just outside Bryson City, the small, secluded lodge is only half a mile from the Great Smoky Mountains National Park, with more than 800 miles of hiking trails, numerous self-guided and ranger-conducted nature walks, and bicycle and horseback trails. The Nantahala River offers white-water rafting, canoeing and kayaking; twenty-nine-mile-long Fontana Lake is great for boating and fishing. Deep Creek, a quarter-mile away, is ideal for the exciting sport of tubing, floating downstream on large innertubes. For shoppers there are several nearby factory outlets, the Mountain Skill-Craft Center (with a large selection of handmade quilts), and an array of area antique shops and flea markets. And the Cherokee Indian Reservation is only ten miles away.

Bob and Irene Kranich are your friendly hosts at attractive, homey Folkestone Lodge, a stone and clapboard farmhouse built in 1926. The lodge, overshadowed by three huge Norwegian spruce trees, sits on four acres of grounds, including woods and some open meadowland. For guests there are six rooms, three of which are on the ground floor. All have double beds and private baths with antique washstands and claw-footed tubs. Each room is tastefully furnished in traditional style with antiques, including high headboards and old hand-crocheted bedspreads. Throughout the house are more country antiques, Oriental rugs and welcoming bowls of fresh fruit.

A family-style breakfast with freshly baked breads is served each morning in the spacious dining room, where floor-to-ceiling windows provide a splendid view of the mountains. The hearty breakfast, which features "Grandma's Old-Fashioned Oatmeal" (a house specialty), homemade sour dough bread, cheese grits, biscuits and gravy, scrambled eggs and ham, homemade jams and perhaps Irene's marvelous cobblers, hot from the oven, is included in the rates; there is also a coffee bar. Guests are invited to enjoy the comfortable parlor

Bed & Breakfast

and library, and in the game room are chess, checkers, cards, dominoes and Ping-Pong. A broad front porch offers rockers and a swing. On the grounds guests may play croquet or horseshoes and wade in the stream with its charming rock bridge; three crystal-clear waterfalls are only a ten-minute walk away. Your hosts even provide backpacking equipment and bicycles to rent.

Folkestone Lodge, Rte. 1, Box 310, W. Deep Creek Rd., Bryson City, NC, 28713; (704)488-2730. (From Bryson City follow the signs to Deep Creek Campground for about 2 miles; watch for the lodge sign on the left.) Rates are moderately expensive, $9 extra per child up to age 16. Children in limited numbers are welcome; no pets, please. Visa and MasterCard are accepted. Please book your reservation including a deposit of one night's lodging or 30%, whichever is greater. There are no wheelchair provisions. Parking available. Open May–Nov. 10.

The Buttonwood Inn. Set amid tall pines, the rustic Buttonwood Inn is in Franklin, an attractive mountain town with an altitude of 2050 feet. The cozy inn, originally a small cottage built in the late 1920s, overlooking the Franklin Golf Course, has been enlarged with the addition of a new guest wing. Owner Liz Oehser has three double rooms for guests, all with private baths, and one suite which includes a twin-bedded bedroom, living room, kitchenette and bath. Three of the rooms are on the ground floor. All of the Buttonwood's rooms are done in tongue-and-groove pine and furnished with a fine collection of antiques and country pieces.

A full breakfast is included in the rates and varies. Culinary delights may include a country breakfast, strawberry omelets, German pancakes or stuffed French toast. Breakfast is served in the dining room; guests are also invited to enjoy the pleasant common room and spacious front porch. The inn's grounds, which adjoin the golf course, offer lovely views of the Nantahala and Cowee mountains and in springtime bloom with dogwood and rhododendron. A deck overlooks a spectacular view.

The golf course offers excellent golfing year-round, and the Franklin area is noted for its ruby, sapphire and garnet mines—great fun for rockhounds.

The Buttonwood Inn, 190 Georgia Rd., Franklin, NC 28734; (704)369-8985. (When you make reservations Liz will provide directions.) Rates are moderate. Well-behaved children are welcome; no pets, please. Parking is available. Open May 15–Oct. 31.

Mountain High. Experience the breathtaking view of five mountain ranges and a beautiful lake at Mountain High, a bed-and-breakfast guest house in Glenville, owned by Mr. and Mrs. George Carter. (The Carters also own Holly Hill, a guest house in Landrum, South Carolina.) Perched on a small ledge below a mountain, the Colonial-style

North Carolina

house stands at an altitude of 4200 feet. There are one single and two double upstairs rooms for guests, with two shared baths. The rooms include lovely handmade quilts, and if you are interested, the Carters will sell you one. Breakfast is included in the rates. All manner of activities are available in the area, including horseback riding and fox hunting. Your hosts, who are experienced riders and masters of the hunt, provide the horses. You will need a car to reach nearby towns for restaurants and shops.

Mountain High, Big Ridge Road, Glenville, NC 28736; (704) 743-3094. (The Carters will give you directions when you call.) Rates are moderate. No smoking. No children or pets, please. Parking is available. Open from approximately June through October.

South Carolina

From its Atlantic beaches and offshore islands to the Blue Ridge Mountains in its northeast corner, South Carolina is a beautiful state. For the vacationer, there's a marvelously diverse assortment of attractions: sports, amusements and festivals of all kinds, an abundance of historic sites and houses, world-renowned gardens and a benign, temperate climate year-round.

Spanish explorers were the first Europeans to visit the region now known as South Carolina, in 1521. Later in that century two coastal colonies were established, one by the Spanish and another by French Huguenots; both were soon abandoned. In 1629, King Charles I of England granted the region, which then included both North Carolina and South Carolina, to a British nobleman, Sir Robert Heath. Heath failed to do anything with it, however, so in 1663 Charles II turned the territory over to a group of eight Lords Proprietors. They later divided the enormous grant into North Carolina and South Carolina.

The first permanent English settlement in South Carolina was founded in 1670 and called Charles Town after the king. (It was renamed Charleston in 1783.) The tiny colony was first located at Albemarle Point on the west bank of the Ashley River. Ten years later it was moved to the present site, a peninsula between the Ashley and Cooper rivers.

Charleston was, from the first, a patrician community of wealthy planters who established a gracious, formal way of life—a New World version of English aristocracy. Inland, settlers from Scotland, Ireland, Wales and Germany struggled with a very different kind of existence, wresting farmland from the rugged, hostile wilderness. The disparity between the two groups created a feeling of rancor, which did not die out until the mid-1800s. Charleston was South Carolina's capital for many years, and although the up-country settlers outnumbered the coastal planters, the power to run the region's affairs lay entirely with the latter. The outlanders felt, with reason, that they were not properly represented. Even though they paid the same taxes, they were virtually ignored and received no help when it was needed—to fight off attacking Indians, for instance.

A truce was called, more or less, during the American Revolution.

Bed & Breakfast

In 1775, Charleston was the first Southern city to defy the English by joining the revolutionary movement. The royal governor was forced to flee, and in 1776 South Carolina adopted the first independent state constitution. The British fleet attacked and captured Charleston in 1780. Although the English held the city for two years, their victory did them little good. Gen. Nathanael Greene's Continental troops, along with South Carolina patriots, kept the British boxed in, unable to move northward to join the other royal forces. Elsewhere in South Carolina, colonists were beating the tar out of the British in the battles of Kings Mountain and Cowpens.

The long-standing hassle over representation between up-country and low-country factions came to a head shortly after the end of the Revolution. The up-country citizens finally won out; in 1786 the capital was moved from Charleston to the geographical center of the state, where the city of Columbia was founded. The move did not end South Carolina's long history of contentiousness concerning unfair taxation, however. The state, its citizens now united, next took on the federal government.

In 1828 John Caldwell Calhoun, then vice president of the United States, wrote an essay called *The South Carolina Exposition*. It opposed the government's tariff policy, which Calhoun felt favored the industrial North over the slave-holding South. The outcome was a compromise between the state and the federal government, and the tariff was reduced. But when Abraham Lincoln was elected president in 1860, South Carolina (led by Calhoun) became the first state to secede from the Union.

A year later, South Carolinians attacked the federal troops at Fort Sumter in Charleston harbor, setting off the Civil War. By 1868, when South Carolina rejoined the Union, the state was a blackened ruin, victim of General Sherman's march to the sea. Not until recent years did it really recover from the economic troubles resulting from the war and its aftermath. A combination of agriculture, a great influx of industry lured by the state's vast waterpower projects, an accessible labor force and low tax rates has turned South Carolina's economy around. Today it is one of the most prosperous states in the South.

Geographically, South Carolina can be divided into three regions: the Up Country of mountains and foothills; the Midlands, a gently rising plateau running down the center of the state, and the Low Country, a flat coastal plain fringed by Atlantic beaches, bays, inlets and sandy offshore islands.

The Low Country

The coastal plain Low Country of South Carolina begins at the northeast tip of the state. The Grand Strand, some sixty miles of broad, sandy beaches, runs along the coast from Myrtle Beach down to Georgetown. All along the way travelers can enjoy warm-water swimming, surfing, fishing, great seafood and a host of family activities. Beginning in Georgetown, founded in 1729, you will find yourself gradually easing into South Carolina's romantic past. Farther south along the coast comes the seaport of Charleston, enchanting with its elegant ambiance, flowers and rows of lovely old houses.

Charleston

If your antennae are at all sensitive, you may note a certain air in Charleston of gentle condescension towards strangers. It is not that Charlestonians are intolerant of visitors; on the contrary, they are extremely gracious, courtly mannered folk who want outsiders to appreciate their charming old city as much as they do. That nebulous air of superiority you perceive is inherited. For Charleston, way back in the 1600s, was established and then governed for a time by the only true aristocracy in American history.

The Lords Proprietors who first ruled the Carolinas set up a feudal system of government complete with four houses of parliament and three orders of nobility. Charleston's aristocratic tradition began with its founder, Anthony Ashley Cooper, Earl of Shaftesbury, and with the dukes, barons and earls who created the region's vast rice and indigo plantations. The idea of a New World British-style nobility, however, did not set too well in the Carolinas—certainly not with the masses of ordinary colonists who emigrated there primarily to get away from that sort of thing. The era of the ruling class lasted less than half a century. But in Charleston, the Ghosts of Nobility Past still lurk in the narrow cobblestone streets and in the old houses standing serenely behind lacy, wrought-iron gates. And their patrician attitudes are still quite discernible in modern-day native Charlestonians. Actually, it's nice—a genial form of *noblesse oblige* towards those of us unfortunate enough not to be Charleston-born and bred.

Charleston is a delightful city for walking. Its streets are shaded by great live oaks adrip with Spanish moss; the air is fragrant with the scents of jasmine, honeysuckle, magnolias and mimosa. After the Civil War, when the disappearance of slave labor brought the day of the great plantations to a close, Charleston fell upon hard times. Over the years many of its historic old houses and other structures fell into disrepair, and only in recent years has renovation been possible. There used to be a common local saying, "too poor to paint, too proud to whitewash," but today a large number of the city's buildings have been restored. A marked walking tour will lead you past a host of eighteenth- and nineteenth-century houses, museums and churches, including Rainbow Row, its fourteen narrow homes all painted in different colors.

The city's Old Slave Mart Museum and Gallery presents the cultural history of the American Negro; Dock Street Theatre, built in 1736 as

Bed & Breakfast

the first structure in America to be used solely for theatrical purposes, has been reconstructed and now offers a winter series of plays. You may also stroll around the grounds of the Citadel, the Military College of South Carolina. On Fridays during the school year, visitors can watch the cadets on dress parade performing colorful precision drills.

If you're not a walker, another pleasant way to see Charleston is to take a tour by horse- or mule-drawn carriage. Narrated bus tours are also available, and a harbor boat tour will take you out to historic Fort Sumter where the first shots were exchanged between the Union and the Confederacy. Details on all tours and walks may be acquired at the Visitor Information Center at 85 Calhoun St.

For a glimpse of how Charleston's long-ago planters lived, drive out to Boone Hall Plantation, eight miles north of the city. Dating back to 1681, Boone Hall was primarily a cotton plantation and covered 17,000 acres. Ancient live oaks line the ¾-mile entrance drive; the original cotton gin house and nine slave houses are still standing. Drayton Hall, nine miles northwest of Charleston, was built in 1738 and is a superb example of Georgian Palladian architecture.

No visitor to Charleston could possibly leave without a trip to one or more of its splendid gardens. Magnolia Plantation and Gardens, ten miles north of the city, were begun in the late 1600s. Today the 30 acres of gardens present a glorious springtime display of camellias, magnolias, a profusion of azaleas and hundreds of other kinds of flowers. The house is open for tours, and there is a petting zoo on the grounds, a miniature-horse ranch and a 150-acre wildlife refuge through which visitors can take a canoe or boat ride.

Middleton Place Gardens, the oldest landscaped gardens in America, were started in 1741. Located fifteen miles northwest of Charleston, Middleton Place is a Tudor mansion built in 1755. The gardens rise from the river in sweeping terraces; paired butterfly lakes lie at their foot. A number of festivals are held on the grounds during the year: a Greek Spring Festival in May, Arthur Middleton's Birthday Celebration in June, Scottish Highland Games in September, a Medieval Lancing Tournament in October and, in November, the harvest-time Plantation Days.

Cypress Gardens, twenty-four miles north of the city, offers 160 acres of water gardens with giant cypresses, azaleas and sub-tropical flowers. Visitors can take a boat trip through the lagoons: the craft floats lazily, silently over black waters that reflect the stately trees and lovely flowers. The gardens were originally a wild cypress forest, which hid the famed "Swamp Fox," Gen. Francis Marion, during the Revolutionary War. The best time to visit Charleston's gardens is in the spring when the azaleas and other flowers are in full bloom. Cypress Gardens are open only from Feb. 15 to May 1. Magnolia Plantation and Middleton Place Gardens are open year-round.

In late May and early June, the city presents the internationally acclaimed Spoleto Festival, U.S.A. The festival, an offshoot of the original, founded in Spoleto, Italy, by the renowned composer-conductor Gian Carlo Menotti, offers a wonderfully comprehensive program of opera, ballet, modern dance, jazz, drama, and symphonic, choral and chamber music. And every spring and fall Charleston opens many of its finest private homes to the public for an assortment of house and garden tours, some of them by candlelight. A number of the city's historic structures also welcome guests, year-round, offering a taste of Charleston's special quality and a great deal of gracious Southern hospitality.

The Sword Gate Inn. Walter E. Barton is the innkeeper at the elegant Sword Gate Inn, one of Charleston's historic eighteenth-century homes. During its long history the mansion has served as a young ladies' seminary and as the British Consulate. George Hopley, the British Consul in 1849, added the famous sword gates for which the house is named. A superb example of wrought-iron art, the gates are designed with two spears joined at the center of a broadsword to form a cross. Hopley also installed the gilded mirrors in the antique-filled, second-floor Grand Ballroom, which guests are invited to tour. The mansion also, so it is said, boasts a resident ghost. Her name, in case you should chance to run into her, is Madame Talvande; she was headmistress of the seminary.

Although the mansion fronts on Legare (pronounced "Legree") Street, the entrance to the inn is on Tradd Street, through a cobbled brick courtyard. There are six guest rooms, four on the ground floor. All have private bathrooms, a double and twin bed, a sitting area, a color TV, a private phone and air conditioning. The individually decorated suites are comfortably furnished and include some antiques such as four-poster and brass beds. Flowers and fresh fruit are also provided. In addition, the inn offers two upstairs rooms, at the very top of the house, with a grand view of the city.

The rates include the morning newspaper and a generous Charleston breakfast served in the elegant dining room adjacent to the ballroom. (Mr. Barton points out that the ballroom is the last in

Bed & Breakfast

Charleston in its original condition. Decorated in the Federal style in 1848, its elegance is characteristic of the Old South.) The breakfast menu varies, but usually includes eggs cooked to order, cheese grits, muffins, fruit and juice. Guests may help themselves to coffee and tea at any hour. Mr. Barton entertains his guests with wine and cheese in the early evening and is always eager to discuss the interesting history of the house. Information on all the local restaurants is available, and Mr. Barton will make recommendations as well as reservations for out-of-town patrons.

The Sword Gate Inn, 111 Tradd St., Charleston, SC 29401; (803) 723-8518. Rates are expensive. No children or pets, please. Parking, off-street, is available. American Express, Visa and MasterCard are accepted. Open year-round except Dec. 24-27.

The Vendue Inn. This inn, owned by Evelyn and Morton Needle, was once one of Charleston's solidly built, old waterfront-area warehouses. Now transformed into an appealing guest house, the inn offers an atmosphere of eighteenth-century elegance and quiet charm. A brick-walled inner courtyard with flowers and greenery provides a cool place to relax. Or, there is a cozy library where guests are invited to enjoy sherry while reading a good book or current periodicals. Afternoon wine and cheese are available, sometimes accompanied by a concert of chamber music performed by local musicians.

There are thirty individually decorated guest rooms and suites, some of which are on the ground floor. All of the accommodations

South Carolina

have private baths, air conditioning and color TV. At night, maids turn down the beds and place a foil-wrapped chocolate on each pillow and liqueurs on the bedside table. A continental breakfast is included in the rate and is served in the Vendue Inn dining room or in your room.

An additional facility available to guests desiring longer stays is the Vendue Inn Carriage House. Located behind Rainbow Row, this eighteenth-century house has a charming living room, kitchen, two bedrooms and a bath. Each room has a wonderful fireplace, and two of the rooms overlook a lovely terraced courtyard.

The Vendue Inn, 19 Vendue Range, Charleston, SC 29401; (803) 577-7970. (Off East Bay Street near the waterfront.) Rates are expensive for all accommodations, lower for longer stays. American Express, Visa and MasterCard are accepted. Children are welcome; no pets, please. Parking is available with security guards after 10 p.m. Open year-round.

The Battery Carriage House. In 1845, Samuel N. Stevens built a house on South Battery Street in Charleston. Twenty-five years later Col. Richard Lathers purchased the place and set about turning the original modest residence into an architectural fashion place. Lathers, a retired millionaire, had returned to South Carolina to help rebuild the state after the Civil War. He hoped that his house would serve "as a meeting place for men of good will, from both the North and the South."

And so it did. In April, 1873, the Charleston *News and Courier* reported a gala evening at the mansion—a party given in honor of Horatio Seymour, ex-governor of New York, and William Cullen Bryant, editor of the *New York Evening Post*. The soiree was described as "one of the most notable social events of the Charleston season," gathering "a most select and fashionable assemblage, including the most prominent gentlemen of the city, with their ladies, as well as a number of military guests from the garrison at the Citadel."

Today the mansion is the home of Frank and Becky Gay, and its elegant ambiance may be shared by guests of good will from every-

Bed & Breakfast

where. Notable for its broad piazzas and ornate wrought-iron gates, the house overlooks the Battery and harbor. There are ten air-conditioned double guest rooms, with private baths, in the beautifully restored carriage house. Six of the rooms are on the ground floor. All are furnished in eighteenth-century style, with wide canopied beds, Oriental rugs and historic Charleston wallpapers and fabrics. The accommodations include phone, color TV, stereo, radio, a fully equipped kitchenette and a concealed wet bar. The last is stocked with soft drinks and a complimentary bottle of wine, replenished daily.

The rates include a continental breakfast of coffee, juice, English muffins laden with strawberry jam, the famous Benedict cheesecake made from a treasured family recipe, or ham croissants, served in your room or in the garden. The brick-walled garden, with wisteria arbor, potted plants, Battery benches and small heated swimming pool, is a delightful place at any time of the day or evening. Your hosts will most likely be on hand in the late afternoon, offering guests a glass of sherry. The Gays also provide bicycles for guests' use, at no charge.

The Battery Carriage House, 20 S. Battery, Charleston, SC 29401; (803) 723-9881. Rates are expensive. American Express, Visa and MasterCard are accepted. Children and pets are welcome. On-street parking is available. Open year-round.

The Elliott House Inn. Built around 1861, the Elliott House Inn stands on one of Charleston's earliest settled plots of land. Part of a three-acre tract known as Schenkingh's Square, the property was later owned by Barnard Elliott, a wealthy planter. The first buildings on the site were erected by William Mills, father of architect Robert Mills, designer of the Washington Monument. In 1866 an earthquake damaged many buildings in Charleston, including the Elliott House. Evidence of the quake may be seen today in the slanting third-floor porch and two second-floor rooms. Earthquake bolts, metal rods running through the walls to provide support, may be noted on the front and side of the old building. A common feature of many Charleston dwellings, they are usually painted black and from the front resemble large buttons.

The modern addition to the inn, constructed on the site of the old slave quarters, is designed in the style of a typical carriage house. Owned by Frank G. Gay, Jr., who also owns and operates Charleston's Battery Carriage House, the inn is managed by Michele Baldrick. There are twenty-six air-conditioned double guest rooms, all with private baths and phones. Ten of the rooms are on the ground floor. Every room includes flowers and a complimentary bottle of imported wine; individual balconies overlook the grounds of the Gibbes Art Gallery and the Charleston Library Society. The rooms are furnished with Oriental rugs and handsome reproductions of eighteenth-

South Carolina

century pieces, including four-poster and canopy beds. Spacious armoires, crafted by a local cabinetmaker, open to hold guests' belongings; each armoire also contains a discretely hidden color TV.

Continental breakfast, included in the rates, consists of orange juice, and your choice of homemade Benedict cheesecake, toasted English muffins or ham croissant, coffee or tea. You may have your breakfast brought to your door on a silver tray, or take it alfresco in the bricked courtyard. The courtyard, with greenery, a charming fountain and heated whirlpool bath, is a cool and peaceful place to enjoy your complimentary champagne or tea each afternoon beginning at 2. Bicycles are available at no charge for guests.

The Elliott House Inn, 78 Queen St., Charleston, SC 29401; (803) 723-1855; toll-free: (800) 845-7638 (out of state); (800) 922-7638 (in state). Rates are expensive; holiday and weekend special package rates are available. American Express, Visa and MasterCard are accepted. Children are welcome; no pets, please. Parking is available across the street in the county parking garage. Open year-round.

Two Meeting Street Inn. A three-story Queen Anne Victorian mansion, Two Meeting Street has been a guest house for more than fifty years! Visitors from all over the world have stayed here, including Princess Anastasia of Russia and Warren G. Harding. The house, completed in 1892, was a wedding gift from George Walton Williams to his daughter when she married into the Carrington family. In the 1930s, the Carringtons began taking in guests, and Mrs. J. H. Carr, who purchased the place in 1946, continued to operate it as a guest house. When she died in 1981 at the age of 90, her nephew, David

Bed & Breakfast

S. Spell, inherited the property and is continuing its tradition of gracious hospitality.

Mr. Spell has completely renovated and restored the spacious mansion, adding central air conditioning, new heating and electrical systems, and updating the plumbing. Furnished throughout with family antiques, Oriental rugs and lovely accessories, Two Meeting Street is an exceptionally elegant inn, with a wealth of fine architectural features. These include turrets and towers, 12-foot sliding doors, high ceilings and windows and seventeenth-century Dutch fireplace tiles. Arched piazzas on two sides face Battery Park; the main floor, with a magnificent staircase, is handsomely paneled in carved oak. Tiffany stained-glass windows grace the living room, foyer and stair landing; a spectacular sunburst window measuring six feet across may be admired in the oval dining room. Your host's collections of silver and old blue and white Canton china are also on view.

For guests there are five large, beautifully appointed bedrooms, with private baths, branching off the upstairs foyer. Two smaller rooms with semi-private baths are on the third floor. Three of the second-floor rooms open onto the upstairs piazza, and two Honeymoon rooms include either access to the piazza or a private balcony. Both have a fireplace, four-poster bed and private bath. Guests are encouraged to enjoy the entire inn, as if it were their own home. Continental breakfast is included in the rates. Sherry is served in the main dining room in the afternoon and evening.

Two Meeting Street Inn, 2 Meeting St. at the Battery, Charleston, SC 29401; (803) 723-7322. Rates are expensive, but a 10% discount is given for stays longer than 7 days (except during holiday periods). Children over 8 are welcome; no pets, please. Parking is available. Open year-round.

South of Charleston, South Carolina's coastline becomes a watery region of inlets, sea marshes and semi-tropical offshore islands. Hilton Head Island, now a popular resort, was discovered in 1663 by the English explorer Capt. William Hilton. Hunting Island State Park offers 5000 acres of beaches, forests and marshes; a 136-foot tall lighthouse may be climbed for a spectacular view of the surrounding area. The Sea Islands region was once renowned for its long-staple cotton, the finest grown in America. Gullah, an intriguing dialect once commonly spoken by many of the islands' black inhabitants, may still be heard occasionally.

Beaufort

Beaufort, on Port Royal Island, is one of South Carolina's prettiest and most historic towns. Spanish explorers discovered its excellent harbor in 1520; the first Protestant colony on the American continent was founded here in 1562 by French Huguenots. Spanish, English and Scottish colonies, all short-lived, followed. The present town was founded in 1710 and named after the British Duke of Beaufort. (Beaufort, by the way, is pronounced locally as "Bu-fort.") Indian wars almost destroyed the town, and the British occupied it during the American Revolution. During the Civil War Union soldiers took over Beaufort, and in doing so, saved the city from General Sherman's disastrous "March to the Sea."

Beaufort's entire downtown area is now listed on the National Register of Historic Sites and includes a large collection of beautifully restored ante-bellum houses and churches, some dating back to the early 1700s. Each April the town hosts a home and garden tour, and in July the picturesque week-long Water Festival takes place along the harbor waterfront.

The Bay Street Inn. A stately house fronting on the water, the inn is owned by Gene and Kathleen Roe. Built in 1852 by Lewis Reeve Sams, a wealthy cotton planter, the house is a superb example of the Barbados-influenced Beaufort style adapted to Greek Revival. Noted for its marble front stairs and wide verandas, the inn sits on a high masonry foundation with a broad view of the Intracoastal Waterway. Used as a hospital by Union officers during the Civil War, the house was recovered by the original family after the war ended. From 1869 until the Murray family purchased the place in 1980, the house belonged to a family named Waterhouse.

For guests, there are five upstairs rooms, all with private baths, air conditioning, fireplaces and views of the water. Each is individually decorated and furnished with antiques. Complimentary sherry, fruit baskets and evening chocolates are included in each room. Guests are invited to enjoy the Roe's music room, living room and library, too. Breakfast, included in the rates, features homemade breads and is served in your room or out in the lovely garden. Guests will also receive a morning newspaper, and the Roes provide bicycles at no charge for visitors to use. Bay Street Inn is in the heart of Beaufort's

Bed & Breakfast

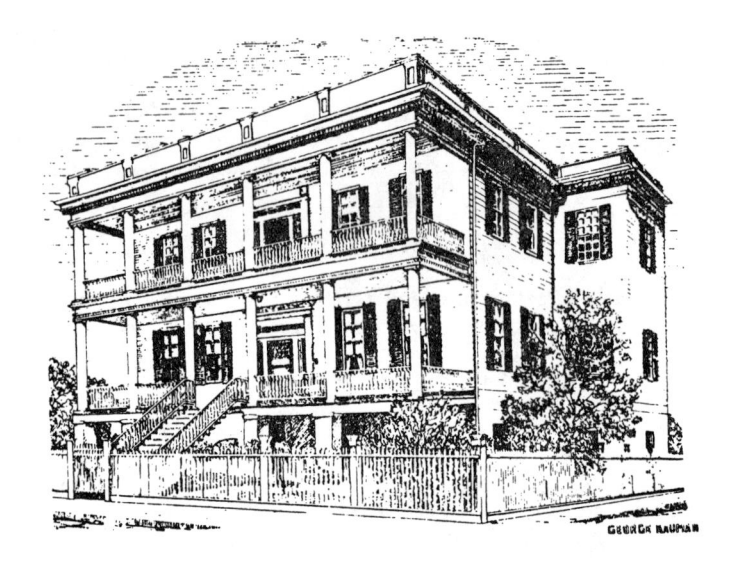

historic district, within walking distance of shops, restaurants and the town's more than 100 historic buildings. Tennis, golf, fishing, hunting and boating are all available nearby; beaches are sixteen miles away. Pickup service is available at the yacht club and airport if pre-arranged.

Bay Street Inn, 601 Bay St., Beaufort, SC 29902; (803) 524-7720. Rates are expensive, lower for longer stays from December through February. MasterCard and Visa are accepted. Children 10 and older are welcome; no pets, please. Off-street parking is available. Open year-round except for August.

The Thomas Rhett House Inn. This elegant Greek Revival restored mansion was built in 1820 by a low-country planter who specialized in sea island cotton. With that in mind, it is interesting to note that a previous owner of the Inn seriously believes that a ghost, a bearded man with a top hat and long coat, inhabits the house. However, your current host, Mr. Bill Long, has yet to encounter such a spirit.

Guests are encouraged to enjoy the patio and fountain, the hot tub in the garden, and the upstairs veranda furnished with Pawley's Island hammocks and wicker pieces. In the den, guests may use the VCR and tape library, and the library which includes classic literature and a grand piano. A complimentary continental breakfast is furnished as well as a bottle of chilled wine, a bedside bottle of sherry, and chocolates for your late-night enjoyment. There are five guest rooms,

South Carolina

two of which share a bath; one of the guest rooms is on the ground floor.

The Thomas Rhett House Inn is located in the historic district, only 200 yards from the Beaufort Marina. It is also within walking distance of several historic places of interest, including the Tidal Home where the movies *The Big Chill* and *The Great Santini* were filmed.

The Thomas Rhett House Inn, 1009 Craven St., Beaufort, SC 29902; (803) 525-1166. Rates are expensive. American Express, Visa and MasterCard accepted. No children under 10 or pets, please. Parking available on the premises. Open year-round.

Tennessee

Colorful Tennessee is a "downhome" state ... a region of rugged beauty, country music and mountain ballads, old-time crafts and sour mash whiskey, and friendly, easy-going people. Long and narrow, the state extends from the rambling Mississippi River and fertile Delta plains in the west to the ancient peaks of the Great Smoky Mountains in the east. More than half of the land is forested, and one of Tennessee's proudest claims is that no matter where you are, a state or national park is within an hour's drive. Outdoor enthusiasts will love the state: the fishing, hunting, boating, skiing, camping, canoeing and hiking are outstanding, and for spelunkers there are more than 2500 caves to explore! In addition, Tennessee offers historic sites galore, exciting cities and, throughout the year, a host of festivals.

Early explorers of the region included Hernando de Soto, back in the mid-1500s; it is believed that the Spanish adventurer visited what is now Memphis. Frenchmen journeyed down the Mississippi River in the 1600s, but no permanent settlements were established in Tennessee until the latter half of the 1700s. Those first intrepid settlers came from the east, traveling over the mountains. Several became American legends.

Daniel Boone made his way from North Carolina, passed through Tennessee and then went on to Kentucky. Andrew Jackson, too, came from North Carolina, but stayed in Tennessee and later served as a United States congressman and senator, as a judge and major general, and finally as the seventh president of the United States. Sam Houston, from Virginia, moved to Tennessee as a boy. Houston ran away from home to live with the Cherokees; as an adult he served in Congress and eventually became governor of Tennessee. Three months after his marriage, however, Houston resigned the governorship, left his wife and rejoined the Indians for a time before finally settling in Texas. Davy Crockett, yet another legendary American hero, was born in Tennessee; he also ended up in Texas—at the Alamo, where he died.

The earliest settlements in Tennessee were established near the mountains, mainly by Scotch-Irish, English and German pioneers, a contentious, free-thinking lot. Although the region was still part of North Carolina at the time, North Carolina's seat of government back

Bed & Breakfast

east refused to protect the settlers from Indian attacks. Instead, the troublesome outlying territory was handed over to the federal government. The indignant settlers retaliated by forming the independent State of Franklin, in 1754. Congress, however, did not recognize the state, so North Carolina took possession once more. In 1788, the State of Franklin was outlawed, and in 1790 North Carolina once again ceded the region, called the "Territory South of the River Ohio," to the United States government. Six years later the territory was admitted to the Union as the State of Tennessee.

During the Civil War, Tennessee saw more fighting than any other state except Virginia. Four National Military Parks have been established on the sites of the bloody battles of Chickamauga and Chattanooga, Fort Donelson, Shiloh and Stones River. In the twentieth century, the state's economic welfare was given a giant boost through the formation of the Tennessee Valley Authority—a massive federal flood control, electrical power and navigation project.

The bill creating the TVA was adopted by Congress and signed by President Franklin D. Roosevelt in May, 1933. From the first, despite claims by private industry that the act was socialistic and unconstitutional, TVA proved enormously successful. A series of stair-step dams along the Tennessee River and its tributaries has controlled the once-frequent flooding and resulting land erosion. Navigation has been facilitated, and a vast amount of inexpensive electrical power has been generated; in addition, the numerous lakes formed by TVA dams now offer some of the best recreational fishing and boating in the country.

West Tennessee

Memphis

Memphis, down at the southwestern corner of the state, is Tennessee's largest city. A thriving, modern metropolis, the old river port still retains much of its Old South ambiance. Visitors can take a riverboat ride on the Mississippi, wander through the superb Memphis Zoo or explore the eighty-eight–acre Memphis Botanic Garden. Other attractions include the Pink Palace Museum, with exhibits pertaining to the region's natural and cultural history; Libertyland, a family theme park, and Chucalissa Indian Village, an archeological site where an ancient Indian temple and several native houses have been uncovered and reconstructed. Graceland, Elvis Presley's mansion, is also in Memphis; the grounds may be toured daily.

The Lowenstein-Long House. Abraham Lowenstein, owner and manager of the Old Lowenstein Department Store, built this home in 1901. It has served many functions since then: the Beethoven Music Club

Tennessee

bought it and held recitals on the first floor while the Bolling-Musser School of Music gave music lessons on the second floor with practice rooms located on the third floor; in 1945, the Elizabeth Club, a boarding house for girls, took ownership; in 1968, it became a pharmacy school fraternity house for the University of Tennessee; sadly, it became neglected and vagrants stripped the house of light fixtures, marble walls, bath fixtures, leather wallpaper, and other irreplaceable furnishings. In 1983, Martha and Charles Long bought the house and began the painstaking process of restoring it to the charm and beauty guests now enjoy. It is listed on the National Register of Historic Places and has been nominated for the Preservation Award given by the Memphis Landmarks Commission.

Five guest rooms are available, all on upper floors of the house. Four of the rooms have private baths. All rooms have ceiling fans and fireplaces. Cable TV is available in the sun room; a pay phone is in the back hall, and laundry facilities are available. A complimentary continental breakfast of juice, coffee, fresh fruit, and coffee cake or sweet rolls is provided. Other meals may be furnished with prior arrangements. A historic restaurant is across the street, but other eating establishments are not within walking distance. Nearby scenic attractions include Graceland, the Pink Palace, Victorian Village and Libertyland.

The Lowenstein-Long House, 217 N. Waldran, Memphis, TN 38105; (901) 274-0509 or (901) 527-7174. (Coming from the west, exit at Front Street and go 1 block south to Poplar, then approximately 1 mile to the guest house parking lot.) Rates are moderately expensive, lower for longer stays. Children are welcome. With advance permission, and only in special circumstances, pets are allowed. Secured, fenced parking available. Open year-round.

Bed & Breakfast

Middle Tennessee

Nashville/Murfreesboro

Nashville, Tennessee's capital, lies approximately in the center of the state. An old city, Nashville was first settled in 1779 as Fort Nashborough. President Andrew Jackson's beautiful home, the Hermitage, is open to visitors; Jackson and his wife are buried in the garden. Another of the city's famous structures is the Parthenon, a replica of the original temple in Athens, Greece. Constructed for the 1897 Tennessee Centennial, the building contains a collection of pre-Columbian artifacts, replicas of the Elgin Marbles and nineteenth- and twentieth-century art.

The famed Natchez Trace, an ancient Indian trail that became the most heavily traveled road in the Old Southwest in the 1800s, once ended at Nashville. Someday the scenic parkway that more or less follows the Trace's original course will be completed all the way from Natchez, Mississippi, to Nashville. Currently, however, it ends at Gordonsburg, south of the city near Columbia. Belle Meade, a gracious plantation house near Nashville, was once a way station on the Trace.

Historic though it is, Nashville's major claim to fame is its music, a tradition that dates back to the 1700s. Two centuries ago, Nashville's early settlers brought with them the mountain music of their homes back east in the Smokies. The Grand Ole Opry began with "hillbilly" music, then developed the "Nashville Sound," a mixture of country and western. Opryland USA, a 120-acre musical theme park, tells the story of American popular music. The site of the new Grand Ole Opry House, the world's largest broadcast studio, Opryland offers more than seventy musical productions daily.

Southeast of Nashville, near Murfreesboro, travelers may tour Stones River National Battlefield. Shiloh National Military Park is just west of Waynesboro, to the southwest.

Clardy's Guest House. Approximately half an hour from Nashville, in the historic city of Murfreesboro, you will find Frank Clardy's guest house, in business since 1954. Built in 1898, and characterized as Victorian Romanesque, this guest house has accommodations decorated in Victorian-period antiques. There are seven guest rooms, three on the ground floor. Three rooms have private baths and four share baths. Guests are invited to relax in the living room, which has a TV, or during the summer, on the large front porch overlooking Main Street with a view of other structures indicative of the lifestyle of the nineteenth century. A complimentary breakfast of coffee, tea and toast is provided. Activities in the area include a pre-Civil War mansion, Oaklands; Stone's River National Military Park; Middle

Tennessee State University; a reconstructed pioneer village, Cannonsburgh; and only thirty miles away, Opryland and Nashville.

Clardy's Guest House, 435 E. Main St., Murfreesboro, TN 37130; (615) 893-6030. (Off I-24, take Exit 78 heading west, toward Nashville; Exit 78B heading east, toward Chattanooga; SR-96 east to Murfreesboro, where Clardy's is 3½ blocks from the public square.) Rates are inexpensive. Children and pets are welcome. Parking available. Open year-round.

East Tennessee

A mountainous region of spectacular beauty, the eastern portion of Tennessee was—in the 1700s—America's first frontier. The Great Smoky Mountains, which extend into North Carolina, are named for the mysterious blue-gray haze that rises from the valleys to the summits. The Cherokees called the region the "Land of a Thousand Smokes." Thousands of acres of forested wilderness offer hiking trails, campsites, great hunting and fishing, and picturesque, small mountain towns where old-time crafts are still practiced by proud mountain people.

Gatlinburg/Chattanooga/Knoxville

Gatlinburg, in the foothills of the Smokies, was once one of these quaint mountain hamlets. Today it is a popular year-round resort, and definitely "touristy." Set in a valley surrounded by wooded peaks and laced with rushing streams, Gatlinburg boasts a wealth of family

Bed & Breakfast

entertainment including ice skating and bobsledding, skiing, golfing and several scenic tramway rides. Scores of shops and studios display locally made crafts (and far too many tacky souvenirs). The handmade items, however, are well worth collecting: quilts, pottery, wooden toys and games, split-oak baskets, dulcimers and lovely hand-woven fabrics.

Nearby Silver Dollar City, a colorful mountain theme park, re-creates pioneer life in the 1870s; Cades Cove, a preserved settlement in a narrow meadowland, also illustrates the mountain way of life as it was a century ago. From Gatlinburg, you can drive up into the Great Smoky Mountains National Park; Clingman's Dome, at 6642 feet the highest point in Tennessee, and Newfound Gap both provide magnificent views. Travelers may see a bear, perhaps several, but are warned to be wary—watch the animals from your car and keep the windows closed.

Southwest of Gatlinburg, the city of Chattanooga has several fine museums, the steepest incline railroad (with a grade near the top of 72.7 percent) in the world, and Lookout Mountain. The area also includes a number of caves which may be explored. Chickamauga and Chattanooga National Military Park, which extends into Georgia, begins nine miles south of the city.

Knoxville, northwest of Gatlinburg, is the home of the University of Tennessee and the headquarters of the Tennessee Valley Authority. In 1982 the city was the site of a World's Fair. A number of historic Knoxville houses may be toured, including the 1792 Gov. William Blount Mansion, the 1797 Ramsey House and the 1830 Speedwell Manor. Within thirty miles of the city you'll find six beautiful TVA lakes for swimming, boating or fishing, and Oak Ridge, "the atomic city" built during World War II by the U.S. government, is just a few miles west of Knoxville. The American Museum of Science and Energy in Oak Ridge contains fascinating exhibits describing the roles of nuclear and other forms of energy in health, power, agriculture, industry and research. Visitors may also examine the famed 1943 Graphite Reactor at the Oak Ridge National Laboratory.

In April Knoxville hosts the Dogwood Arts Festival, a week-long celebration with more than 200 events and activities including flower and art shows, garden tours, parades, sports and theatrical events, and concerts. Some fifty miles of marked dogwood trails may be followed, self-guided or on free bus tours.

Tn. Southern Hospitality, Inc. Headquartered in Knoxville, Katie Reily's bed-and-breakfast organization offers a number of private homes with accommodations for travelers. The lodgings are located primarily in Knoxville, but also include one in Rutledge and one in Maryville, Tennessee. Ms. Reily started Southern Hospitality as a service for visitors to the 1982 World's Fair. She says: "These homes and their owners withstood a countless number of World's Fair guests, of all types and at all hours—and they came out like champs!"

A sampling of the listings includes a suburban home three miles from downtown Knoxville with a guest bedroom offering a king-size waterbed, two single beds and one crib. Closed off from the rest of the house, the room (with private bath) has its own entrance and a deck that overlooks a swimming pool. In Maryville, about twenty minutes from the entrance to the Great Smoky Mountains National Park, an entire top level of a house is available for guests. A simple home in a lovely country setting, the house includes three bedrooms, a living room, dining room, fully-equipped kitchen and private bath for guests' use. In Rutledge, forty miles east of Knoxville, a Southern-style red-brick house built in 1847 and used as a hospital for Confederate soldiers during the Civil War includes beautiful antiques and a free-standing staircase. Five bedrooms and three baths are available for guests.

Contact: Tn. Southern Hospitality, Inc., P.O. Box 9411, Knoxville, TN 37920; (615) 577-8363. Suitable accommodations will be chosen for you, and you'll be sent a confirmation and directions to the house. Rates are inexpensive, lower for a clean, simple room and perhaps a shared bath, a bit higher for a deluxe room with private bath. A small added charge is made for a third person in room; children under 5 are free.

Kingsport/Rogersville

Northeast of Knoxville, Kingsport is way up near the border of Virginia. The Great Indian Warrior and Trader Path and Island Road, Tennessee's first constructed road (later to become the Great Stage Road) was built in 1761 and passed through Kingsport. Situated on the Holston River, the city is today a major industrial site; Kingsport Press, one of the world's largest producers of books, is located here. At Boat Yard Park on the river, visitors will enjoy a tour of the historic Netherland Inn, once a famous stop on the Great Stage Road. The boatyard complex also includes picnic areas, fishing and boating facilities, and a children's museum.

West of Kingsport is the historic town of Rogersville. One of the oldest towns in Tennessee, it has become an outstanding cultural center in the South.

The Hale Springs Inn. Rogersville, nestled between the Holston River and the Clinch Mountain range, is the setting for the Hale Springs Inn. This inn, circa 1824–25, was built by John McKinney (originally it was called McKinney's Tavern) and was host to many famous personalities. President Andrew Jackson once lived at the Inn. Presidents Andrew Johnson and James K. Polk also were guests. The Inn became Union headquarters during the Civil War, rather appropriately since it faces north to the motherland. In 1982, the Inn

Bed & Breakfast

was purchased by Capt. Carl Netherland-Brown, formerly master of the liner S.S. *Bahama Star.* Under his direction, extensive restoration has retained the splendor of this oldest continuously run inn in the state of Tennessee.

Seven guest rooms are available, plus two suites. All rooms are on the second and third floors and have private baths. The rooms are very large with individual sitting areas, but guests may also feel free to use the lobby area for relaxing. Included in the standard rates is a continental breakfast of coffee, juice and Danish. Soft drinks, coffee and tea are available at any time. Guests are within walking distance to shopping and restaurants within the Rogersville Historic District, and the Inn has its own restaurant. Travelers are sixty-five miles east of Knoxville and thirty miles west of Kingsport.

The Hale Springs Inn, 110 W. Main St., Rogersville, TN 37857; (615) 272-5171. (Write for a brochure which includes rates, directions and activities.) Rates range from moderate to expensive. American Express, Visa and MasterCard are accepted. Children are welcome; no pets, please. Parking available at the Inn. Open year-round.

Virginia and Washington, D.C.

History is irresistible in the Old Dominion State of Virginia. There is scarcely an inch of ground that does not tell a story, from seventeenth-century Jamestown and the pre-Revolutionary capital of Williamsburg to Civil War battlegrounds. The state abounds in historic sites and buildings, including a host of stately plantation homes where visitors are offered a fascinating glimpse into Virginia's aristocratic past. A stunningly beautiful state, Virginia stretches from the Tidewater Region and Eastern Shore to the lovely Shenandoah Valley and ancient mountain highlands.

In 1584, Sir Walter Raleigh sent a small band of English explorers to investigate the region. The expedition named the territory Virginia for Elizabeth, England's Virgin Queen. But it was not until 1607 that Virginia's real history—and that of our nation—began. In May of that year, Jamestown, the first permanent English colony in America, was founded on the banks of the James River. The settlement was established by the London Company under a grant from King James I and was named, as was the river, for him.

In 1624, England revoked Virginia's charter and made it a royal colony, ruled directly by the crown through a royal governor. England's imposition of burdensome taxes, as well as other highhanded acts, began to create resentment among the colonists. The Indians, too, were causing problems by attacking outlying settlers in a series of savage raids. In 1676, when Gov. William Berkeley refused to help the settlers, a planter named Nathaniel Bacon formed an army of colonists. Bacon and his men marched on the Indians, defeating them soundly. Governor Berkeley, instead of being grateful for the intervention, proclaimed Bacon to be a "rebel." Feeling that Jamestown was the seat of British oppression, Bacon twice marched on the capital, burning it on his second visit. Shortly thereafter he died of malaria and his "rebellion," a forerunner of the American Revolution, collapsed.

In the latter part of the following century, Virginia once again led the other colonies in resistance to the crown. Her royal governor was

Bed & Breakfast

driven out in 1775, and several Virginians including George Washington, Patrick Henry and Thomas Jefferson became Revolutionary leaders. In 1778, after the war ended, Virginia was the tenth state to join the Union. Prior to the Civil War, the state at first opposed secession and changed its stance only when President Lincoln sent out a call for troops. Robert E. Lee, another famous Virginian, resigned his commission in the U.S. Army to become commander-in-chief of the Confederate forces, and during the war Virginia was one of the major battlegrounds of the Confederacy. The state was readmitted to the Union in 1870. After surviving the difficult Reconstruction years, Virginia went on to become one of the South's most progressive states.

Northeastern Virginia
Washington, D.C.

The northeastern portion of Virginia and our nation's capital, separated only by the Potomac River, share much of the same history. Part of the District of Columbia, in fact, once belonged to Virginia. A beautiful city of wide, tree-lined streets, imposing government buildings and a fabulous collection of museums, Washington was designed in 1791 by Maj. Pierre Charles L'Enfant, working under the supervision of President George Washington. L'Enfant's plan for the new capital is still considered remarkable today—a gridiron pattern of north and south streets, diagonal avenues and the magnificent park called the Mall, with the Capitol Building as the focal point.

Wonderful though it is to see, however, Washington is not a joy for motorists. L'Enfant's design was not meant for twentieth-century automobile traffic; even the residents find the streets confusing to negotiate in a car, and parking is a real problem. The easiest way to get around is via the excellent subway system, the Metro. Or, you can take one of the many sightseeing tours available. A good place to begin exploring is the National Visitor Center on Massachusetts Avenue at First Street, N.E., in the restored Union Station Building. Knowledgeable personnel will supply information and brochures, and help organize your stay. The following are some of Washington's most-visited sites:

The U.S. Capitol, Capitol Hill. Construction began on the Capitol in 1793, but the building was not finished until 1867. During those years it was enlarged a number of times, and completely rebuilt after the British burned it in 1814.

The U.S. Supreme Court. Just behind the Capitol, the Supreme Court Building was completed in 1935. The impressive courtroom is open to the public and interpretive tours are offered.

Library of Congress. Located next to the Supreme Court Building,

Virginia & Washington D.C.

the Library of Congress was established in 1800. The British burned it, too, during the War of 1812, and the Library had to start its collection all over again. Thomas Jefferson aided the cause by contributing about 6500 volumes. Today the building houses some 73 million books, manuscripts, recordings, maps and prints, photographs and other materials, including such priceless treasures as a Gutenberg Bible.

Folger Shakespeare Library. Containing one of the world's finest collections of Shakespearean and English Renaissance books, the Folger Shakespeare Library is behind the Library of Congress.

The National Archives. Situated between Pennsylvania and Constitution avenues, the National Archives includes the original Declaration of Independence, the Constitution and Bill of Rights, and others of our nation's most historic documents.

National Gallery of Art. On Constitution Avenue, the National Gallery houses art treasures from the thirteenth to the twentieth century.

Smithsonian Institution. The Smithsonian, on the Mall, contains an incredible number of items, encompassing practically all of human culture. The museum's buildings include the National Portrait Gallery, the National Collection of Fine Arts, the Freer Gallery of Art and Renwick Gallery, the Hirshhorn Museum and Sculpture Garden, the National Museum of Natural History, the National Museum of History and Technology and the National Air and Space Museum.

The White House. The nation's most famous house lies beyond the Ellipse, at 1600 Pennsylvania Ave. Eleven of its rooms are open for morning tours from Tuesday through Saturday. The gracious mansion has been the official residence of every American president except George Washington. After being burned by the British in 1814, the house was restored and painted white—thus its name.

The Washington Monument. On the other side of the Ellipse, visitors may climb 898 steps or take an elevator to the top of the Washington Monument. The 555-foot-tall obelisk was first opened to the public in 1888.

The Lincoln Memorial. At the end of the Mall next to the Potomac, the Lincoln Memorial was sculpted by Daniel Chester French, who also created the famous Minuteman Statue in Concord, Massachusetts. Washington residents often stop late at night on their way home, just to pay homage to the remarkably moving marble figure.

The Thomas Jefferson Memorial. On the south bank of the Tidal Basin, a large bronze statue of Jefferson, third President of the United States, reposes in a classically styled temple. In early April, the hundreds of cherry trees that surround the memorial and the Tidal Basin burst into bloom. The trees were a gift to the city of Washington from the mayor of Tokyo, Japan, in 1912.

Ford's Theatre. In 1865, President Abraham Lincoln was assassi-

Bed & Breakfast

nated at Ford's Theatre. The building, at 511 Tenth St., N.W., has been authentically restored and includes a Lincoln museum. Theatrical performances are held in the theater throughout the year. The house in which Lincoln died, at 516 Tenth St., is also open to visitors.

Georgetown. Home of Georgetown University, established in 1789, Georgetown is a colorful mixture of lovely old houses, steep narrow streets and numerous interesting shops and restaurants.

The John F. Kennedy Center for the Performing Arts. The Kennedy Center is at New Hampshire Avenue and F Street, N.W., not far from the Lincoln Memorial. Our national cultural center includes an opera house, concert hall and movie and drama theaters; guided tours are offered.

Washington churches. The city's notable churches include the National Shrine of the Immaculate Conception, the nation's largest Roman Catholic church, on Michigan Avenue, N.E.; the Franciscan Monastery, with replicas of such great Christian shrines as the Grotto at Lourdes and the Garden of Gethsemane, at 1400 Quincy St., N.E., and Washington National Cathedral, a Gothic-style Episcopal cathedral begun in 1907 and still under construction.

National Zoological Park. The main entrance to the zoo is on Connecticut Avenue, N.W., in the 3000 block. Great fun for the whole family, the zoo includes a spectacular outdoor aviary and a pool full of noisy sea lions. Among the approximately 2500 creatures on display are such famous animals as Smokey the Bear and the two giant pandas from China.

The Kalorama Guest House at Kalorama Park. In three charming Victorian townhouses, the Kalorama is in the fashionable embassy district on one of the city's prettiest streets. Elegant Connecticut Avenue stores are close by for shopping or browsing; Columbia Road's ethnic restaurants, night spots and antique shops are a block away, and the Washington Hilton Convention Center is a few minutes' walk. The White House, the Capitol Building and the Mall are all within two miles, and the Woodley Park Metro stop is just across the Calvert Bridge for easy access to the airport and downtown Washington.

Roberta ("Birdie") Pieczenik owns the Kalorama Guest House; Mr. Jim Mench is the resident manager. Built circa 1800 as a single-family residence, the structure later served as a rooming house. In the early 1980s the handsome old townhouse was restored and transformed into a delightful bed-and-breakfast establishment in the European tradition. For guests there are twenty-three attractive rooms, including singles, doubles and triples. Some share baths; others have private baths. Each room has its own sink. Two large, bay-windowed rooms include a separate dressing room, and one room has a private porch overlooking Kalorama Park. The guest quarters are decorated in period style with brass beds, Oriental rugs, turn-of-the-century artwork, wing chairs and several 100-year-old rockers. As Mrs. Pieczenik says: "There's nothing plastic or laminated; the furniture is all wood!" In addition, the rooms are graced with the original mantels, plush comforters, live plants, plenty of reading lamps and closet space and a nice assortment of Victorian bric-a-brac, plus books and magazines to read. Each room also includes a desk and radio-alarm clock.

Breakfast, included in the rates and served in the dining room, consists of juice, a choice of pastries and coffee or tea. In the afternoon, the upstairs parlor is an inviting spot to enjoy a glass of complimentary sherry—beside a crackling fire if the weather is chilly. Local phone calls are free; a coin telephone is provided for long-distance calls, and there is a twenty-four-hour answering service for messages. A washer/dryer is available on the lower level. Also, there is a lovely, enclosed yard where guests may relax.

The Kalorama Guest House at Kalorama Park, 1854 Mintwood Place, N.W., Washington, D.C. 20009; (202) 667-6369. (Three blocks off Connecticut Avenue between 19th St. and Columbia Road.) Rates are moderate to moderately expensive, lower for weekly or longer stays. American Express, MasterCard, Visa and Diners Club are accepted. No cigars, please. Children are welcome; no pets, please. Two parking spaces are available at the house for a $3 per night charge. Otherwise, ask your host for directions to a parking lot or garage. Open year-round.

The Kalorama Guest House at Woodley Park. In true Kalorama Guest House tradition, your hostess, Roberta ("Birdie") Pieczenik, and her manager, Rick Fenstemaker, have opened the Woodley Park location, only twelve blocks away from Mintwood Place. Guests may expect the same high standards of excellence that they have enjoyed at the Kalorama Park location. At Woodley Park, there are nineteen rooms, some with private baths, housed in two quaint Victorian

Bed & Breakfast

townhouses. Seven of these guest rooms are on the ground floor, and three have private baths.

A complimentary breakfast of orange juice, coffee, tea, cocoa, croissants, English muffins, raisin bread and a wide selection of toppings awaits guests in the dining room each morning. Coffee is always available, and there is sherry on the buffet. Guests are invited to relax in the several living and dining rooms, use the games and relax on the outdoor patio.

The Woodley Park Metro stop is two blocks away; the National Zoo is one block, and Connecticut Avenue is one block.

The Kalorama Guest House at Woodley Park, 2700 Cathedral Ave., N.W., Washington, D.C. 20008; (202) 328-0860. Rates are moderate to moderately expensive, lower for weekly or longer stays. American Express, Visa, Diners Club and MasterCard are accepted. Children are welcome. No pets or cigars, please. There are 2 parking spaces available at the house at $4 per night. Otherwise, ask your host for directions to a parking lot or garage. Open year-round.

Arlington/Alexandria/Fredericksburg/Orange

Arlington National Cemetery is just across the Potomac, in Virginia. Established in 1864, the 420-acre site contains some 174,000 graves; most of those buried here were members of the U.S. armed forces killed in battle. Numerous monuments may be seen, including the Tomb of the Unknown Soldier, now called the Tomb of the Unknowns, and the Marine Corps Memorial Iwo Jima Statue, which depicts the 1945 raising of the American flag on Mt. Suribachi. Among the many famous Americans buried at Arlington are President John F. Kennedy and his brother Robert, President William Howard Taft, Adm. Robert E. Peary and generals George C. Marshall and John J. Pershing. Also on the cemetery grounds is the Custis-Lee Mansion, with a splendid view of Washington from its columned portico. The Greek Revival house was built in 1817 by George Washington's foster son, George Washington Parke Custis. Custis's daughter married Robert E. Lee, and the Lee family lived here until 1861.

At Great Falls Park, about fifteen miles from Washington, the Potomac River cascades over tumbled masses of rock in a series of dramatic waterfalls; there are hiking trails and picnic areas, too. A word of warning: don't try to climb out on the rocks; the swift water makes them very slippery and dangerous. Alexandria, south of Arlington, includes a restored Old Town and waterfront area with more than a thousand historic houses. The Alexandria Tourist Council at 221 King St. offers a walking tour map and a fourteen-minute film entitled "Alexandria in Virginia—George Washington's Town." When Washington was only 17 and an apprentice surveyor, he helped lay out and map the town's streets.

Along the walking tour are Carlyle House, built in 1752; a 1792

Virginia & Washington D.C.

apothecary shop, now a museum of early pharmacy; the home of Gen. Henry (Lighthorse Harry) Lee, the 1785 Lee-Fendall House; Robert E. Lee's boyhood home; Gadsby's Tavern, dating to the 1770s and often visited by George Washington; and several churches, including Christ Church, which contains family pews that once belonged to Washington and Lee. Another Alexandria building, not on the tour, is the George Washington Masonic National Memorial. The 33-foot-tall structure, patterned after the ancient lighthouse in Alexandria, Egypt, looms over the city from atop Shooter's Hill rather like a brooding giant—a memorable, and indescribably ugly, sight.

To erase its bulk from your mind, head next for one or more of the magnificent plantations in the area. Woodlawn, seven miles south of Alexandria, was completed in 1805. George Washington gave the land, 2000 acres, to his foster daughter Nellie Custis as a wedding present in 1799. Washington's own home, Mount Vernon, is a few miles away. The oldest part of the house was built around 1735 by Washington's father; George brought his bride, Martha, here in 1759, and they are both buried on the grounds. The mansion, a beautifully proportioned white Colonial, sits high on a bluff overlooking the Potomac. From its columned, two-story piazza there is a glorious view over sweeping lawns down to the river below.

George Washington died in 1799, Martha a few years later. A nephew, Bushrod Washington, inherited the property. But by the 1830s the estate had become unproductive; its buildings were falling into disrepair, and gardens and grounds were neglected. In 1853, an enterprising woman named Ann Pamela Cunningham formed the Mount Vernon Ladies' Association. The group purchased the mansion and restored it over the next twenty-five years. Amazingly, Mount Vernon survived the Civil War; as a sort of neutral zone between the opposing forces, the house was respectfully visited by both Northern and Southern troops.

Another elegant plantation home is Gunston Hall, about nineteen miles south of Alexandria. George Mason, author of the Fairfax Resolves (which served as the model for the Bill of Rights), lived very comfortably here, surrounded by a collection of exquisite furnishings. The red-brick mansion was built in the late 1750s; its classic boxwood gardens are renowned. Manassas (Bull Run) National Battlefield Park is also located in this northeastern Virginia area, twenty-six miles southwest of Washington. Two major Civil War battles were fought here, and more than 23,000 men were killed or wounded. Self-guided tours begin at the Visitor Center, and there is a museum with an audio-visual presentation and exhibits.

If you have the time, drive down to Fredericksburg, approximately fifty miles south of Alexandria. Or, plan to pay it a visit on your way to Williamsburg and Jamestown. The chamber of commerce proudly calls Fredericksburg "America's Most Historic City." George Washington went to school here, and his sister lived in a handsome Georgian

Bed & Breakfast

brick manor house in the town. Washington's mother is buried in Fredericksburg's old cemetery; other famous residents have included James Monroe and Commodore John Paul Jones.

Situated on the Rappahannock River, Fredericksburg was a major port until the 1850s when the railroads drained off most of its shipping traffic. Then, because of the town's strategic location between Richmond and Washington, Fredericksburg became a viciously contested prize during the Civil War, changing hands seven times. Four major battles, fought in and around the town between 1862 and 1864, left it badly damaged. Somehow, many of its eighteenth-century buildings managed to survive and may be visited today. Walking or driving tours originate at the Visitor Center, a charming 1817 house with a garden courtyard. Fredericksburg and Spotsylvania National Military Park, just west of the town, includes parts of all four Civil War battlefields. The engagements—the battles of Fredericksburg, Chancellorsville, Spotsylvania Court House and the Battle of the Wilderness—involved the bloodiest, most concentrated fighting ever to take place on American soil.

Orange, about thirty miles west of Fredericksburg, is a town of presidents and more Civil War battlefields. The James Madison home, Montpelier, and the James Madison Museum are two "musts" for tourists.

Hidden Inn. Owner Doris Rosback offers more than just a room for the night. The atmosphere at Hidden Inn is warm and inviting during the winter with a fire crackling in the living room fireplace, and it's cool and relaxing in the summer on the veranda that wraps around the inn . . . and everything is "family style." Ms. Rosback has furnished the five guest rooms for pleasure and comfort. Handmade quilts, by a local artist, adorn many of the beds, and there are furnishings brought back from trips to Europe. Of particular interest is a ceramic cook stove used as a buffet. Two rooms have private baths; one guest room is on the ground floor and has a half bath and fireplace. There is a TV in the living room and a well-stocked library. The house is Victorian, circa 1900, and is nestled on five acres filled with walnut, oak, tulip, maple and pine trees. Montpelier is only three miles away, and Monticello is close by in Charlottesville. Antiquing and visits to nearby wineries make for full days of activity.

A full breakfast, featuring special pancakes, is included in the rates. Afternoon tea is served, if desired.

Hidden Inn, 249 Caroline St. (Rte. 15), Orange, VA 22960; (703) 672-3625. (From Washington, D.C., and the beltway, I-495, take I-66 west to US-29; US-29 south to Culpeper; US-15 from Culpeper to Orange.) Rates are moderately expensive; there is no charge for small children in their parent's room. Visa and MasterCard are accepted. Children welcome; no pets, please. Parking available. Open year-round.

Tidewater Region

The Tidewater is Virginia's inner coastal region, a low, flattish area with a ragged shoreline marked by innumerable bays and inlets. The state's great tidal rivers—the Potomac, Rappahannock, York and James—flow through the region into vast Chesapeake Bay. The Bay separates the Tidewater region from Virginia's Eastern Shore, a long, narrow peninsula that connects with Maryland to the north. Historic Jamestown, Williamsburg and Yorktown are all located in the Tidewater area.

Richmond

Richmond is a bit west of the Tidewater, but it's a good place to begin your exploration of the region. Virginia's capital since 1780, Richmond was also the capital of the Confederacy. In 1865, fleeing Confederate troops started a conflagration that destroyed a large portion of the city. A few ante-bellum buildings survived the fire, including the State Capitol and Governor's Mansion; St. Paul's, St. John's and St. Peter's churches; Robert E. Lee's wartime home, and the 1790 John Marshall house.

Southeast of Richmond, a number of lovely old plantations lie along the James River. Many of the magnificent houses and their grounds and gardens are open to the public. For maps and information, ask at the Metropolitan Richmond Convention and Visitors Bureau, 201 E. Franklin St. Route 5 leads first to Shirley Plantation, about twenty miles from Richmond. Built between 1723 and 1770, it has been the home for nine generations of the Carter family. Berkeley

Bed & Breakfast

Plantation, built by Benjamin Harrison IV in 1726, is about three miles farther. Benjamin Harrison V, signer of the Declaration of Independence, and William Henry Harrison, our ninth president, were born here. Then comes Westover, constructed around 1730 by Richmond's founder, William Byrd II, and Sherwood Forest, notable for its 300-foot-long mansion—one of the longest private dwellings in America.

Over on the other side of the river is Brandon Plantation, a 440-acre estate with spectacular gardens. Bacon's Castle in Surry County is farther along, on Route 617, off Route 10. Built in 1655, the Castle is the last surviving manor house in America constructed in Jacobean style. It was the home of Nathaniel Bacon, that seventeenth-century "rebel" against English rule.

The Catlin-Abbott House. The Catlin-Abbott House, in Richmond's historic Church Hill district, was built in 1845 for William Catlin by his slave, William Mitchell. Mitchell, who was the father of Maggie Walker, the first woman bank president in the country, was one of

the finest brick masons of his time. The Catlins hired him out to construct other buildings in the area. In 1850, Mr. Catlin moved down the street to another house which was built as a wedding present for his third wife, Rebecca.

A six-room addition, in which the present owners, Dr. and Mrs. James L. Abbott, now live, was built in 1870 to accommodate boarders. (Loss of property and fortunes during the Civil War forced many genteel families of the old South to take in roomers.) The Abbotts purchased the house in 1980. Previously, they lived in Hagerstown,

Virginia & Washington D.C.

Maryland, where Frances Abbott, a widow from Richmond, had moved when she married orthodontist James Abbott. There she turned their restored 1845 fieldstone farmhouse into an inn. Homesick for Richmond, however, she was delighted when her husband suggested relocating in Virginia. Discovering that the old Catlin house in Richmond was for sale, they bought the place and proceeded to have it restored. The structure was in sad shape, boarded up and gutted, with walls stripped to the brick and floorboards missing from one of the bedrooms. In 1982 the renamed Catlin-Abbott House, a splendid example of the Federal style, once again opened its doors to guests as a charming bed-and-breakfast establishment.

There are five double rooms for guests: one with a private bath on the top floor, two on the second floor sharing a bath, and a suite with two bedrooms, bath, kitchen and private patio on the basement level. Guests also have the use of the house's living room, dining room and veranda. Four of the bedrooms have working fireplaces, and the entire house has been furnished by Frances Abbott with lovely antiques and reproductions, including four-poster beds and Chinese rugs. Wake-up coffee is brought to your room each morning, and a full breakfast, included in the rates, is served either in your room or in the elegant dining room. The breakfast menu varies and may include fruit or juice, coffee or tea, eggs with bacon or sausage, home fries and grits, or "Dr. Jim's Fabulous Pancakes."

Many of Richmond's historic sites are within walking distance of the house: St. John's Church, where Patrick Henry uttered the famous words "Give me liberty, or give me death!" is just one block away.

The Catlin-Abbott House, 2304 E. Broad St., Richmond, VA 23323; (804) 780-3746. Rates range from moderately expensive to expensive, with a 10% discount for longer stays. American Express, Visa and MasterCard are accepted. No children or pets, please. Street parking is available. Open year-round.

Jamestown/Mathews/Williamsburg/Yorktown

These three historic sites are all southeast of Richmond. The most scenic way to reach them is to follow Route 5 or routes 10 and 31, past the James River plantations. For the proper historical perspective, stop first at Jamestown Colonial National Historical Park, on the Colonial Parkway off Route 231.

Jamestown, founded in 1607, was beset by difficulties from the start: crops failed, the Indians were hostile, and the damp, swampy surroundings fostered malaria and other illnesses. And as if the problem of sheer survival were not enough, the colonists bickered constantly among themselves. Capt. John Smith, a remarkably able and resourceful man, soon became the group's leader and managed to create some order among the settlers. He also organized trade with the Indians, at some risk to himself. Smith was captured by Chief

Bed & Breakfast

Powhatan and saved from death by Pocahontas, the chief's daughter. Pocahontas later married John Rolfe, another Jamestown settler.

Smith returned to England in October, 1609; during the following winter the colony almost went under. Its population was cut almost in half; the "starving time," as that period was called, reduced the number of inhabitants from 104 to about 60. But an influx of new settlers and supplies in 1610 brought new hope, and Jamestown finally began to prosper. The colonists even managed to achieve an impressive number of firsts: they made glass in 1608, began growing tobacco commercially four years later, and in 1619 the first representative assembly in America was held in the town. Jamestown also had the dubious distinction of being the destination of the first black slaves brought to this country from Africa.

In 1699, after the town had suffered several fires, the colonial government moved to nearby Williamsburg. Jamestown was virtually abandoned, and eventually died out altogether. Today, the only remains of the colony are the foundations of several buildings, an old church tower and traces of streets and boundaries unearthed in archeological explorations by the National Park Service. The Park Service and the Association for the Preservation of Virginia Antiquities have provided markers and recorded talks that tell Jamestown's story; the Visitor Center offers exhibits and a film.

Adjacent Jamestown Festival Park is a re-creation of the seventeenth-century colony and includes John Smith's fort, Powhatan's lodge, thatched cottages and full-scale replicas of the three ships that brought the colonists from England—the *Susan Constant*, *Godspeed* and *Discovery*. Exhibits in the Old World (British) and New World (American) pavilions depict the background and chief events of the colony's early years.

Now follow the Colonial Parkway six miles to Williamsburg. The town, situated on a peninsula between the York and James rivers, was first settled in 1633 as Middle Plantation, an outpost against Indian attacks. When Virginia's seat of government was moved here from Jamestown in 1699, the town was renamed for England's King William III. Williamsburg is also the home of the College of William and Mary. Founded in 1693, the college is the second oldest in the country; only Harvard is older.

Williamsburg quickly became the center of Virginia's political, cultural and social life. The bustling Colonial capital almost boiled over during the twice yearly "publick times" when the legislature met and courts were in session. At those times the town's population doubled; its visitors crowded the inns and taverns and enjoyed a wealth of entertainment, including fairs, horse races, banquets and elegant balls. But in 1870, Virginia's capital was once again moved, this time to Richmond. And Williamsburg, its historical importance almost forgotten, drowsed on for a century and a half. During those years many of the original buildings decayed or, even worse, were

Virginia & Washington D.C.

torn down and replaced by newer structures. Then, in the 1920s, wealthy philanthropist John D. Rockefeller entered the picture. Inspired by Dr. W. A. R. Goodwin, rector of Bruton Parish Church, Rockefeller financed an awesome undertaking—the restoration of Colonial Williamsburg.

To date, the project has cost close to $100 million; architects, historians, landscape gardeners, archeologists, town planners, builders and many other experts have contributed their talents to the restoration. The restored area (only a small portion of the actual town of Williamsburg) is about one mile long and half a mile wide. Within these boundaries approximately 600 buildings were moved or razed. Some 88 of the original structures have been preserved and restored, and about 50 buildings, among them the Capitol and Governor's Palace, have been rebuilt upon the original foundations. Gardens have been replanted with care, and authentic furnishings acquired for the houses.

Today, Colonial Williamsburg lives again, complete with the sights and sounds (but, thankfully, not the smells) of 200 years ago. "Townsfolk" in typical Colonial attire go about their business—plying their trades, serving meals in the colorful old taverns, driving horsedrawn carriages and wagons or simply stopping to chat awhile with visitors. Tours begin at the Colonial Williamsburg Information Center, with an introductory thirty-five-minute film. There is a special tour just for youngsters and evening candlelight tours, too.

The Duke of Gloucester Street is the main thoroughfare; the Capitol building, where Patrick Henry gave his rousing speech against the Stamp Act, is at the east end, and the College of William and Mary is at the west end. In between are the Raleigh Tavern and Wetherburn's Tavern, the Public Gaol, the handsome Governor's Palace and Gardens, Bruton Parish Church, the Courthouse of 1770, and many interesting houses and craft shops. As you roam you can munch on a freshly baked cooky or spicy gingerbread or stop for a meal in one of the taverns once patronized by such notables as Thomas Jefferson, Patrick Henry and George Washington.

From mid-March to early October, visitors may watch an exciting militia muster presented twice weekly on Market Square Green or, on Saturdays from April to November, a fife and drum corps parade. Throughout the year all manner of special events take place, including art exhibitions, Colonial fairs and theatrical performances. At Christmastime, Williamsburg celebrates the festive season with carols, dancing, candlelighting ceremonies and fireworks.

The Colonial Parkway next takes you east to Yorktown, on the York River. First settled in the 1630s, the village was officially founded in 1691. A thriving seaport up until the mid-1700s, in 1781 Yorktown was the scene of the final action of the American Revolution. The British general Lord Cornwallis and his men were trapped in the town, surrounded by American and French forces under Gen. George

Bed & Breakfast

Washington. Cornwallis surrendered after a siege that lasted twenty days. Peace was not officially declared for another two years, but the British defeat brought an end to the war's actual battles. Visitors to Yorktown may explore the battlefield, the Moore House, Swan Tavern and other old buildings. Carter's Grove, six miles southeast of Williamsburg on 60, is one of the most beautiful of all the James River plantations. The house, built between 1750 and 1753, is open to the public; the pewter collection is especially outstanding.

Right on the Chesapeake Bay is the village of Mathews with its historical attractions and beach.

Riverfront House. Within an hour of Williamsburg and Busch Gardens, Riverfront House is in Bay Country, an area of peace and beauty. Annette Waldman Goldreyer invites you to enjoy her circa 1840 farmhouse surrounded by fruit trees and daffodils, at one time a major crop of the area. There are five guest rooms (one on the ground floor) with newly installed semi-private bathrooms, and one third-floor room has a private bath. Guests are invited to enjoy the large living room and dining room, furnished with Victorian pieces.

There is also a wraparound veranda with a screened porch and a picnic table, a private dock (for crabbing!) and seven unspoiled acres to roam. Guests may moor their private boats at the dock; hike or bike five miles to the Mathews beach; or enjoy the historical village of Mathews with its flea markets and antique and craft shops. Included in the rate is a continental breakfast featuring fresh, locally grown fruits; muffins, bread or Danish; breakfast cheese and coffee or tea. *Riverfront House, Rte. 14 East, P.O. Box 310, Mathews, VA 23109. (Rte. 17 south through Saluda to Glenns, V-198 east from Glenns to Mathews. In Mathews, turn right on Rte. 14 east for .9 mile. You'll go through the village to a sign on the right for Riverfront House; third entrance after bus shelter.) Rates are moderate with a 10% discount for three or more nights. Children are welcome on weekdays, but no toddlers, please. No pets, please. Parking available. Open late April to early November.*

Virginia & Washington D.C.

Williamsburg Inn Colonial Houses. In the restored Historic Area of Colonial Williamsburg, more than a score of Colonial homes, shops, taverns and cottages offer guest facilities for travelers. Operated by the famed Williamsburg Inn, these unique accommodations range from a large sixteen-room brick tavern to a tiny cottage tucked away in a garden. All are beautifully furnished in authentic eighteenth-century style and are absolutely delightful. They are also expensive. But staying in any one of the lodgings will be well worth the cost if you're feeling extravagant; it's like going back 200 years in time, yet having all modern conveniences. (Inquire as to whether breakfast is served at the location of your choice.) Within easy walking distance of the Williamsburg Inn, the Colonial Houses receive its full services.

For information, write to Reservations Manager, Colonial Williamsburg Foundation, P.O. Box B, Williamsburg, VA 23187, or call toll-free (800) 446-8956; local, (804) 229-1000. Advance reservations are recommended, and a deposit of the first night's room rate is required. Rates are very expensive. Children are welcome; no pets, please. Parking is available. Open year-round.

Hampton/Newport News/Norfolk/ Portsmouth/Virginia Beach

Southeast from Williamsburg is a cluster of seaport towns: Hampton, Newport News, Norfolk and Portsmouth. Virginia Beach, a popular resort area, lies just beyond. Venerable Hampton's history began when the Jamestown colony sent some of its men here in 1610 to cultivate the area's abundantly growing wild grapes. Although James-

Bed & Breakfast

town was founded three years earlier, Hampton claims the honor of being the oldest English settlement in America still in existence. A self-guided driving tour will take you to St. John's Church, built in 1728; Kicotan Indian Village, a re-creation of seventeenth-century Indian life, and Fort Monroe. Jefferson Davis was once imprisoned in one of the fort's casements, a chamber in the fort walls.

Newport News, Norfolk and Portsmouth make up the Port of Hampton Roads, one of the world's finest natural harbors and the scene of the famous 1862 battle of the ironclads *Monitor* and *Merrimac*. Take a harbor cruise from any of the three towns to see some of the area's vast shipping and ship-building operations. The Museum in Newport News houses a fine collection of nautical articles, including ship models, figureheads, paintings and prints. In Norfolk, travelers may tour the Naval Base; the Gen. Douglas MacArthur Memorial; the Chrysler Museum, with a stunning collection of Titians, Renoirs and other masterpieces; the Norfolk Botanical Gardens, and Lafayette Zoo. Portsmouth, connected with Norfolk by tunnels and bridges, is famed for its historic houses and the Naval Shipyard Museum.

Virginia's Dismal Swamp lies a bit south of the Portsmouth/Norfolk area. The eerie swamp stretches for about forty miles in a long, narrow ribbon of trembling peat. Lake Drummond in its center, reachable by boat, is an eighteen-square-mile expanse of amber-colored water. Because the lake's water retained its sweet freshness for so long, it was once highly prized for use aboard ships. For sun and saltwater fun Virginia Beach, just east of Portsmouth, offers twenty-eight miles of white sand beach, great swimming and fishing and a host of other sports activities and amusements.

Angie's Guest Cottage. Located right in the heart of Virginia Beach, Angie's Guest Cottage has a fine view of the ocean from its sun deck. Barbara Yates and her parents, Bob and Garnette Yates, operate the place. Accommodations include four single and/or double rooms, one triple, and one room that sleeps four or five. There are also two apartments that sleep up to four comfortably. Five rooms share two centrally located baths; one room offers a private bath, as do both apartments. Five of the rooms are on the ground floor. In addition, the Yateses have added two rooms to accommodate backpackers and bicyclists and are affiliated with AYH, Inc. The fee is $9.72 for members and $12.96 for non-members (space available). The hostel attracts travelers from around the world giving guests the opportunity to meet interesting people from different nations!

The rooms and apartments are all decorated to make guests feel right at home. One room opens directly onto the sun deck. All have good, firm beds and are air conditioned; some include small refrigerators for snacks and cold drinks. TV sets are available upon request. The apartments are large efficiencies with eat-in, fully equipped kitchens. Guests are invited to enjoy the sun deck, the front porch

Virginia & Washington D.C.

and a fenced-in back yard with barbecue pit and picnic tables. During the summer breakfast is served daily to room guests. The atmosphere at Angie's is casual, friendly and family style.

The house is one short block from the beach, and 1½ hours from Colonial Williamsburg. Your hosts will gladly tell you about all the interesting sights and activities in the area, including tips on the best restaurants. And in case you're wondering who the "Angie" in Angie's Guest Cottage was, Barbara's family bought the place from her in the late 1970s. As she had developed such a fine reputation, with lots of repeat business, and because "Angie" begins with an "A" (for telephone book and other listings), they decided to keep the name.

Angie's Guest Cottage, 302 24th St., Virginia Beach, VA 23451; (804) 428-4690. (At the intersection of 24th Street and Pacific Avenue, 11 miles from the exit of the Chesapeake Bay Bridge Tunnel, Rte. 13, and 2 blocks from Rte. 44. The Greyhound Bus Station is just across the way.) Rates are moderate and vary according to the room; lower off season. Visa and MasterCard are accepted. Well-behaved children and small pets are welcome. Parking is available in the driveway and on the street. Open April 1–Oct. 15.

The Eastern Shore

In 1614, when the first settlers arrived on the peninsula now known as Virginia's Eastern Shore, they kept its Indian name of Accawmacke, "Land beyond the waters." Life on the peninsula was very different from that of the aristocratic Tidewater with its baronial plantations. The inhabitants of the Eastern Shore led a simpler existence: they fished and farmed and built small villages much like those on Cape Cod, Massachusetts. Even today fishing and farming are the major occupations, and the picturesque towns are still Colonial in appearance and character. The region's windswept beaches and sandy barrier islands, too, seem to resist the passage of time. This tranquil, unhurried region offers wonderful swimming and fishing, and some of the finest seafood in the world.

Bed & Breakfast

To reach the Eastern Shore from Virginia Beach or Norfolk, follow the blue and white signs marked with a sea gull to the Chesapeake Bay Bridge Tunnel. A 17.6-mile stretch of road, the impressive highway runs through two mile-long tunnels and over 12 miles of trestled roadway and 2 miles of causeway, two long bridges and four man-made islands.

Assateague and Chincoteague Islands

The islands of Assateague and Chincoteague are up at the northern end of the peninsula. Assateague includes both the Virginia portion of the Assateague Island National Seashore and the Chincoteague National Wildlife Refuge. It is also the home of those famous wild ponies described so charmingly in Marguerite Henry's book, *Misty of Chincoteague*. Actually stunted horses, the animals' size has dwindled over the years from their diet of marsh grass. When young, they are about the size of a large dog; when full grown the ponies resemble large Shetlands.

According to legend, the horses first came to Assateague about 400 years ago, swimming ashore from the wreck of a Spanish galleon. Every July the animals are rounded up and swum across the channel to Chincoteague Island for "penning." The ensuing week-long festival includes pony rides, carnivals, delicious Chincoteague oysters and freshly caught crabs and clams to eat and an auction in which the wild foals are sold. The remaining ponies swim back to Assateague, where they are allowed to roam freely the rest of the year.

Miss Molly's Inn. In 1886, Mr. J. R. Rowley, then known as "The Clam King of the World," built this charming Victorian home on

Virginia & Washington D.C.

Chincoteague Island. His daughter, "Miss Molly," was one of the island's best-loved citizens, and she lived in the house until the age of eighty-four. While rocking on the front porch with Miss Molly and Captain Jack, Marguerite Henry formulated the plot of her beloved book, *Misty of Chincoteague.* Today, Dr. and Mrs. James C. Stam strive for a family atmosphere at their inn. Thirteen upper-level guest rooms are available, two with private baths. Rooms are air conditioned and furnished in period antiques. The room rate includes afternoon tea and a light breakfast of juice, fresh fruit, quiche, croissant and coffee or tea. Chincoteague has a mystique all its own; as poet Rachel Field reflects: "But—once you have slept on an island, you'll never be quite the same!" Miss Molly's Inn is a fine setting in which to experience this mystique.

Miss Molly's Inn, 113 N. Main St., Chincoteague Island, VA 23336; (804) 336-6686. (US-113 to Rte. 175; east to Main Street in Chincoteague; turn left and go 2½ blocks.) Rates are expensive, with a 12% discount for weekly, and longer, stays. Children over 12 are welcome, but no pets, please. Parking available. Open April 1–Dec. 1.

The Year of the Horse Inn. During the annual roundup, the ponies are paraded right past this delightful guest house on Chincoteague Island! Owned by Carlton and Jean Bond, the Year of the Horse Inn overlooks Chincoteague Bay. For guests there are one efficiency with two double beds, a room with queen-size bed, and a private two-bedroom apartment. All of the large air-conditioned rooms include private baths and balconies, and cable TV. No rooms are on the ground floor. Guests are welcome to share the attractive lobby with its interesting collection of antiques and contemporary pieces that combine to create a "Sidney Greenstreet" ambiance. The latest addition is Kiss the Camel, a four-foot rocking camel with a ceramic "kissy-face." He was acquired from a local art gallery and, according to Mrs. Bond, thoroughly enjoys all the attention he receives from friends and guests.

Included in the rates is a continental breakfast of fresh fruit, homemade cinnamon rolls, coffee and tea which can be enjoyed in the lobby or on the private deck overlooking the Intracoastal Waterway. The grounds also have a picnic area and a private pier where guests may dock their boats. The house is one block from the carnival grounds and close to the Assateague National Wildlife Refuge with its superb beaches, the Atlantic Ocean, hiking and biking trails, birds galore and those wonderful wild ponies. The fishing is great, too. Chincoteague, in addition to all of its other attractions, is known as the flounder fishing capital of the world.

The Year of the Horse Inn, 600 S. Main St., Chincoteague Island, VA 23336; (804) 336-3221. Rates are moderately expensive, lower in the winter months. Visa and MasterCard are accepted. Children are welcome; no pets, please. Parking is available. Closed December and January.

Bed & Breakfast

Virginia's Mountains
The Shenandoah Valley/ Winchester/Mt. Jackson

The Blue Ridge Mountains of Virginia lie just west of the state's central Piedmont Plateau. Beyond them stretches the Great Valley, which separates the Blue Ridge from the Allegheny range. There are actually five valleys: the Shenandoah, through which flows the beautiful Shenandoah River, is the northernmost. During the Civil War the lovely, fertile Shenandoah Valley became a bloody battlefield, fought over time and time again by the opposing armies of the North and South.

Winchester, at the top of the valley, was originally a Shawnee Indian camping ground. The town was first settled in 1732, by a group of Pennsylvania Quakers. In 1748, Thomas, Lord Fairfax, hired the young George Washington to survey some land in the area. Washington spent three years at the job, working out of an office in Winchester. By the Civil War years, the town had become an important transportation center and a prize of great value to both Northern and Southern forces. Winchester changed hands more than seventy times (thirteen, it is said, in one day), and some six battles and more than 100 minor skirmishes were fought in the vicinity.

Today Winchester is the center of Virginia's apple-growing region and home of the Shenandoah Apple Blossom Festival, held each May. An auto tour of the town leads to several historic cemeteries and churches; Gen. "Stonewall" Jackson's Headquarters, where he lived during the winter of 1861–1862; Gen. Phillip H. Sheridan's Headquarters (during the fall and winter of 1864–1865), and George Washington's Office, which now houses a museum.

South of Winchester, near Woodstock, is the town of Mt. Jackson in the heart of the Shenandoah Valley.

Widow Kip's Guest House. Rosemary Kip describes her guest house in Mt. Jackson as a visiting-grandma-type Colonial farmhouse nestled on seven acres overlooking the Shenandoah Mountains. There are six bedrooms, two on the ground floor, all with fireplaces. Three bathrooms are shared. The entire house is filled with antiques and collectibles, all of which are for sale. Memories are everywhere you look.

Widow Kip's offers life at a gentler pace—you can laze by the swimming pool, picnic on the grounds, enjoy a book by the fire, or rock and daydream on the "Lillian Gish" side veranda. If you prefer a faster pace, you can attend area auctions, hike, fish, canoe, ski, visit craft fairs, golf, play tennis and explore caverns. Begin each day with a full country breakfast of juice, coffee or tea; homemade sausage or

Virginia & Washington D.C.

bacon; scrambled eggs; muffins, rolls and toast; apple butter and jams, all included in the rate. The Shenandoah River is a stone's throw away on the Widow Kip's property, and a picnic lunch will be provided if you wish.

Widow Kip's Guest House, Rte. 1, Box 117, Mt. Jackson, VA 22842; (703) 477-2400 or (202) 462-5800. (From I-81 take Mt. Jackson Exit 69 to US-11, south; go 1.3 miles and turn right onto Rte. 263 and then take the second left on Rte. 698. The Widow Kip's is the second house on the left.) Rates are moderate, with lower rates for off-season, extended stays, and children. Visa card is accepted. Children over 7 are welcome, but no pets, please. Parking available. Open year-round.

Upperville/Middleburg/Sperryville

Southeast of Winchester, Upperville is close to both the Shenandoah and Potomac rivers; historic Harper's Ferry is only a short drive away. Middleburg, a charming little village, lies in the center of Virginia's famed hunt country. The Piedmont Hunt is the oldest in America. Sperryville, southwest of Middleburg and just off the Skyline Drive, offers beautiful countryside, antiques and crafts. All three towns, and Winchester, too, are an easy drive from Washington, D.C.

1763 Inn. The fifty acres surrounding the 1763 Inn offer more than just spectacular views. In addition to fishing and hiking, the surrounding horse country features fox hunting, the famous Virginia Steeplechase Races, and the nationally famous Upperville Horse Show. The circa 1763 stone house was once owned by George Washington, and it was raided frequently by Union soldiers during the Civil War. Uta Kirchner has recently renovated the Inn, reflecting a country style. There are six guest rooms in the renovated stone barn, four on the ground floor, and all have private baths. Five of the guest rooms have

Bed & Breakfast

fireplaces and all are rustic and include antiques. All rooms have sitting areas, but Ms. Kirchner encourages guests to enjoy the fireplace in the lobby area or the large, outside patio. Tennis courts are also on the property.

A hearty breakfast of steak and eggs, homefries, juice, coffee and bread is included in the rates. For late arrivals, wine and cheese are served between 6 and 7 p.m. Coffee and tea are available at any time. The Inn is only one hour from Washington, D.C., and thirty minutes from Skyline Drive; Sky Meadows State Park adjoining The Appalachian Trail is only five minutes away.

1763 Inn, Rte. 1, Box 19D, Upperville, VA 22176; (703) 592-3848. (A map is included on the brochure.) Rates are expensive, lower in the off season, June 15–Aug. 1. Special rates for longer stays. American Express, Visa and MasterCard are accepted. Children are welcome. Pets are allowed provided they are attended by the guest at all times. Parking available. Open year-round.

Welbourne. Set on a 600-acre farm in the heart of the Virginia hunt country near Middleburg, Welbourne is one of the most beautiful Southern mansions you may ever see. Mrs. N. H. Morison, a descendant of an early owner of the house, and her son Nat and his wife, Sherry, are your gracious hosts.

The core of Welbourne is a four-storied stone house built around 1775. In 1818, John P. Dulany purchased the place and greatly enlarged it, creating a classic ante-bellum stuccoed brick manor house fronted by a wide piazza with tall, slender pillars. Several of the still existing dependencies were built at the same time, in the same manner, the brick coming from a kiln on the property. Mr. Dulany had previously lived four miles away on a farm known as Old Welbourne, a property that remained in the family for two centuries, from 1750 to 1950. The old family cemetery is still there.

John Dulany's son, Richard, grew up at Welbourne. In 1840, he founded America's oldest hunt, the Piedmont Hunt, and in 1853 he established the Upperville Colt and Horse Show, also the country's oldest. During the Civil War, Dulany served as a colonel in the 7th Virginia Cavalry, and Welbourne was the scene of a score of exciting wartime incidents. The Morisons will be delighted to share some of the stories with you, including tales of burying silver in the garden, hiding Southern soldiers in water tanks and in a large bed full of Dulany children, and a miraculous escape by Colonel Dulany on a splendid jumping horse. The Colonel lost a gauntlet while fleeing; Northern soldiers crushed blackberries on it and told the children of the family that their father had gotten away but had been badly wounded—thus the "bloodstains" on the glove. One of the Colonel's daughters, however, on examining the gauntlet closely, said that it was the first time she'd ever seen blood with seeds in it!

During the last six months of the war all the barns on the property were burned and the livestock carried off. The Dulany children gave food and water to passing Southern troops, and—in brave defiance—sat on the fence and hollered "Hurrah for General Lee!" as the Northern troops passed by. Colonel Dulany, though wounded three times, survived the war and came home to rebuild the family fortunes. He died in 1906 and his second daughter, Fanny, inherited Welbourne. She had nine daughters, the oldest of whom, another Fanny, became owner in 1928. Her great-grandchildren, who now live here, represent Welbourne's seventh generation.

In the 1930s, another of the Colonel's granddaughters became a great friend of Maxwell Perkins, the renowned Scribner's editor of books by Thomas Wolfe, F. Scott Fitzgerald, James Jones, Marjorie

Bed & Breakfast

Rawlings and Ernest Hemingway, among other notables. Perkins once said after a visit to Welbourne that he felt as if he had "... seen an enchanted place." He also sent Wolfe and Fitzgerald for visits; both writers later commented on the vivid impressions they received. Fitzgerald even wrote a short story based on Welbourne, called "Her Last Case," which was published in 1934 in the *Saturday Evening Post*. In a letter, Max Perkins described Fitzgerald's reactions to his stay: "He was fascinated with the quality of that place, and thought the house was haunted with the old South."

Today's fortunate guests at Welbourne are offered eight beautifully decorated upstairs bedrooms in the spacious main house, including one single and seven double rooms. In addition, three cottages on the grounds also accommodate guests: one sleeps two, and two sleep four persons. All but one of the rooms include private baths; some have working fireplaces. Guests are also invited to enjoy Welbourne's antique-filled sitting room and broad porches; the Morisons make a point of welcoming visitors as though they were old friends, offering the finest of warm Southern hospitality. A lavish Southern-style breakfast is included in the rates, served in the magnificently appointed dining room or, if you wish, on a tray in your room. There will be juice, eggs or pancakes, bacon or sausage, grits, fried tomatoes or fried apples, muffins and coffee, tea, or milk. Other meals may be available at additional cost, if requested far in advance.

Surrounded by sweeping, tree-shaded lawns and fields, Welbourne is close to a golf course, the Middleburg and Orange Hunts, the Blue Ridge Mountains and Skyline Drive. The pretty village of Middleburg, with many shops and restaurants, is six miles away; Harper's Ferry is a short drive, and Washington, D.C., is fifty miles away.

Welbourne, Middleburg, VA 22117; (703) 687-3201. (From blinker light in Middleburg, continue west on Rte. 50 for 3½ miles; turn right on Rte. 611 and go 1½ miles; turn left on Rte. 743; Welbourne is 1.2 miles on the left.) Rates are expensive; 10% off for one-week stay, 20% off for two-week stay and 50% off for three-week stay. Children are welcome; pets are allowed, but please be aware that the Morisons have dogs, too. Parking is available. Open year-round.

The Conyers House. A bed-and-breakfast inn of great charm, the Conyers House is in rural Sperryville. Hosts Norman and Sandra Cartwright-Brown, who purchased the property in 1979, began welcoming guests in 1981.

The oldest part of the structure, now the living room/library, was built around 1780; later it was moved to its present location and attached to an 1810 farmhouse. The deed of the old Baptist church next door, dated 1815, refers to Conyer's Old Store, and one of the guestrooms is named for Bartholomew Conyers, the storekeeper. Sandra, who is an amazingly energetic, creative person, claims to recycle everything, and the Conyers House bears ample evidence of this. It is filled with a fascinating collection of items gathered in the family's travels in Europe, Africa and the United States, plus family heirlooms. Antiques, including eighteenth-century plates and needlework, are displayed along with mounted zebra and caribou heads, a rococo mirror purchased from the Ambassador of Malawi, paintings and prints, a Scottish grandfather clock, Oriental rugs and many reborn items culled from Goodwill, country auctions and white elephant sales. The effect is marvelous, thanks to Sandra's excellent taste and decorating skill.

The guest rooms in the main house include Grampie's Room, with a four-poster queen-size bed and heirloom crocheted spread, an antique rocker and working fireplace; Betsy's Room, small and cozy with a four-poster double bed; Helen's Room, with an 1820 rope bed and "bawdy red" wallpaper; Uncle Sim Wright's Room, with a double bed, enormous German armoire and working fireplace; and the Cellar Kitchen with 18-inch-thick stone walls, an 1820 waist-high double bed, a large fireplace in which meals were prepared, an antique wardrobe and a private porch and entrance. The Nicholson Room shares a bathroom with the Cellar Kitchen on weekends. The Nicholson Room has a king-size bed which can be made into twins, a sink and French doors opening onto a private porch and entrance. (During the week, five rooms, with private baths, are available. The Hill House, separate from the main house, offers additional accommodations, but it is available on weekends only.)

The animals at the inn are part of the charm. Pepper, an elderly cock-a-poo, has been joined by Winchester (a young Jack Russell) who will quickly persuade you to throw a stone, apple or stick which he will persistently retrieve. Chelsea is the sleek, aristocratic and

Bed & Breakfast

talkative black semi-Siamese who is very attentive and totally impervious to anyone's dislike of cats. A hearty breakfast, included in the rate, consists of cheese strata, a platter of fresh fruit, bread pudding (to entice you to try Mrs. Woodward's cream) and red pepper jelly to top a cream cheese–slathered English muffin. Afternoon tea, also included, features the housekeeper's parsnip cake (when in season) or applesauce cake. The housekeeper, Debbie Racer, is famous for her fresh trout country dinners—an elegant five-course affair, available by reservation at $25 per person.

Sandra is an avid fox hunter, and the entrance hall resembles a tack room. Guests are encouraged to go on a two-hour trail ride through the magnificent Rappahannock scenery. The Conyers House is in the midst of the Blue Ridge foothills. Climbing Old Rag Mountain is a favorite pastime, as is antiquing.

The Conyers House, 157 Slate Mills Rd. (Rte. 707), Sperryville, VA 22740; (703) 987-8025. (When you make reservations, the Cartwright-Browns will send a map with directions.) Rates are expensive. Children rarely come; they must be old enough to remember that Pepper, the dog, is afraid of small people. Pets may stay in the Hill House, but not in the Main House since the two resident male dogs feel compelled to mark their territory when visiting canines are present. Parking is available. Open year-round.

Virginia's Skyline Drive/Charlottesville

Virginia's famed Skyline Drive begins at Front Royal, about nineteen miles south of Winchester, and winds for 105 spectacular miles through Shenandoah National Park. Curving in gentle grades along the crest of the Blue Ridge Mountains, the parkway offers breathtaking views, particularly in the spring when the apple trees, dogwood and rhododendron are in bloom. Travelers may stop to hike, ride horseback, picnic or fish along the way. Two handsome lodges provide traditional Southern food, and several mountain craft gift shops display a wide variety of handmade items. The area also includes a number of fascinating caverns to explore. Luray Caverns on Route 211, ten minutes from the Skyline's central entrance, are the largest in eastern America. Blasé types are fond of saying that if you've seen one cave you've seen them all, but Luray's underground marvels are really impressive—and vast. Wear comfortable shoes, as you will be doing a lot of walking, and carry a sweater; the caverns are damp and chilly. And remember: stalactites grow downward, stalagmites grow upward.

Charlottesville, just east of the end of the Skyline Drive, is an ideal place to stop and stay for a day or so. Set in the rolling hills below the Blue Ridge Mountains, Charlottesville is Thomas Jefferson's hometown and the site of his handsome mansion, Monticello. Jefferson began building the house in 1769; it took forty years to complete. Perched atop a small mountain, the graciously classical structure is

Virginia & Washington D.C.

surrounded by charming gardens. The thirty-five-room house seems deceptively small from the front; Jefferson created this effect by designing the second-story windows to appear to be part of those on the ground-floor level. Instead of following the custom of the time of constructing separate outbuildings for servants, supplies and various functions, he included a complex of twelve concealed underground rooms for those purposes.

Jefferson believed in labor-saving devices, too, and Monticello is full of them. There are glass double doors that swing open in unison when either of them is opened; the doors are operated by a system of hidden chains. A wall panel in the dining room is a revolving buffet; servants would load it from the outside with dishes from the kitchens below. Dumbwaiters concealed in the mantelpiece brought wine from the cellar. And these are only a few of the countless innovations incorporated into the house.

An awesomely knowledgeable man, Jefferson was a Renaissance American—with an interest in virtually every subject. His brilliance was wittily described by President John F. Kennedy at a dinner for a group of Nobel laureates. Kennedy praised his guests as "the most extraordinary collection of talents . . . that has ever gathered together at the White House, with the possible exception of when Thomas Jefferson dined alone." Jefferson died at Monticello on July 4, 1826, exactly fifty years after the signing of the Declaration of Independence.

You will also want to walk around the University of Virginia's grounds in Charlottesville; the beautiful brick buildings and walls are further examples of Jefferson's architectural genius. Ash Lawn, located five miles southeast of Charlottesville, is another. Jefferson planned the house and its gardens for James Monroe in 1798.

Oxbridge Inn. Formerly known as the English Inn, this grand establishment is located in the heart of Charlottesville's University district and is within minutes of the University of Virginia campus, shops and restaurants. A spacious brick Colonial built at the turn of the century, the bed-and-breakfast inn is owned by Stuart and Anna Klee. There are eight comfortable bedrooms for guests, including one single and five doubles, and two family rooms suitable for three or four persons. Three of the rooms are on the ground floor. One room offers a private bath; three more baths are shared. For relaxing, there are an attractive sitting room, with fireplace for winter use; games, books and TV; a typical "Southern" veranda for summertime; and a large garden. Continental breakfast, included in the rates, consists of juice, homemade breads and sweets, coffee or tea. Monticello and Ash Lawn; Castle Hill, a 1765 plantation with an 1824 addition; and Swannanoa, a Renaissance palace constructed in 1912, are all within easy driving distance.

Oxbridge Inn, 316 14th St., N.W., Charlottesville, VA 22903; (804)

Bed & Breakfast

295-7707. Rates are moderate, lower from November to April. Visa and MasterCard are accepted. Well-behaved older children are welcome; no babies, please. Only small dogs are allowed. Parking is available. Open year-round.

The Blue Ridge Parkway and Virginia's Highlands

The magnificent Blue Ridge Parkway, which begins near Charlottesville at the end of the Skyline Drive, extends for 469 miles all the way to the Great Smoky Mountains National Park in North Carolina. Along the way are turnoffs to such historic Virginia towns as Lexington, Lynchburg and Appomattox. The state's rugged Highlands region lies to the southwest, beyond the parkway. A densely forested area, the Highlands offers mountain lakes and streams, hiking trails and excellent fishing and hunting.

At Big Stone Gap, summertime visitors may watch an exciting drama called *The Trail of the Lonesome Pine*, an outdoor musical version of John Fox's classic novel about life in the Highlands. The famed Barter Theatre, now the State Theatre of Virginia, is in Abingdon. In the 1930s, during the Depression, a Virginia native named Robert Porterfield came home to these mountains, bringing with him a troupe of Broadway artists. The actors performed in return for hams, vegetables, homemade jam—whatever the audience had to offer. At Cumberland Gap, travelers can stand with one foot in Virginia and the other in Kentucky, with a view of four states, including North Carolina and Tennessee.

Lexington/Warm Springs/Hot Springs

Lexington, about fifty miles southwest of Charlottesville, is a charming little town. Washington and Lee University, founded in 1749, and the prestigious Virginia Military Institute, founded in 1839, are both in Lexington, and Confederate generals Robert E. Lee and Thomas J. "Stonewall" Jackson are buried here. Several tours may be followed: one covers some of the highlights of Lee's and Jackson's lives, and another leads through the grounds of the Virginia Military Institute. A third, the Residential Walking Tour, encompasses Lexington's restored downtown area and some twenty-four historic homes. Information and brochures on all of these may be acquired at the Visitor Center, 107 East Washington St. In early December the town presents "Holiday in Lexington," with several days of parades, tours of traditionally decorated shops and houses, candlelighting ceremonies and caroling.

A thirteen-mile drive south of Lexington on Route 11 will bring you to Virginia's Natural Bridge. A massive, 215-foot-high limestone

Virginia & Washington D.C.

arch, the natural bridge is 90 feet long and widens to 150 feet in some places. The roadway runs right over the bridge, spanning two mountains. Long ago, Indians worshipped the bridge; in 1750 George Washington cut his initials in it, and in 1774 Thomas Jefferson was so taken by the stone arch that he bought it! Jefferson paid King George III of England twenty shillings for the bridge, gorge and all. He then hired caretakers and built a visitor's cabin nearby.

Northwest of Lexington are the villages of Warm Springs and Hot Springs, set amid mountains and meadows and offering superb golf, horseback riding, mineral springs and even wintertime skiing and skating.

106 McDowell Street West. Mrs. Lee L. Nichols, Sr., is your cordial hostess at 106 McDowell in Lexington. Her charming house, which looks much like an English or Irish cottage, was built in 1935 of native stones called "river-jacks." It sits back from the street, with a large old magnolia tree on one side of the center flagstone walk and a flowering plum on the other side of the yard. The attractive plantings include boxwoods and evergreens, with ivy borders.

There are four rooms for guests: three doubles, each with twin beds, and one triple with twin beds. Three of the rooms include a private bath, and one semi-private bath is at the end of the second-floor hall. One room, with bath, is on the ground floor. All are furnished with a mix of antiques and country pieces; comfortable upholstered chairs and nice accessories add to the pleasant ambiance. Guests may also share the porch and the spacious living room with a stone fireplace at one end, Oriental rugs, old prints and watercolors and a black-and-white TV.

A full Southern breakfast is included in the rates. Mrs. Nichols offers her guests juice, scrambled eggs with sausage and apples (or hash, if requested), spoon bread or sweet rolls, and coffee or tea. On occasion, if guests prefer, she even provides quiche or eggs Benedict.
106 McDowell St., Lexington, VA 24450; (703) 463-5227. (Turn right off Rte. 11 South, S. Jefferson Street, into one-way McDowell Street; the house is ½ block down.) Rates are moderate. No children under 12 or pets, please. Parking is available. Open year-round except from Dec. 15 through Jan. 5.

Mrs. Hunter McCormick/Guests. A frame house built in the 1920s, with a white-columned front porch and small yard, this Lexington home offers guests four upstairs rooms with two shared baths. All of the rooms are double or triple. Your hostess, Mrs. Hunter McCormick, invites guests to enjoy her reception hall (with a piano), books and Oriental rugs, and the living room with an antique loveseat and matching chairs, marble-top tables, a walnut writing desk and a music cabinet. A continental breakfast of toast and jelly or sweet rolls, and coffee or tea, is included in the rates.
Mrs. Hunter McCormick/Guests, 220 W. Washington St., Lexington, VA 24450;

Bed & Breakfast

(703) 463-3247. Rates are inexpensive. Children are welcome; no pets, please. Parking is available at a nearby lot. Open year-round.

Meadow Lane Lodge. Set on a 1600-acre estate just west of Warm Springs, Meadow Lane Lodge is an outstandingly attractive small country inn. Owned by Philip and Catherine Hirsh, the lodge is a white Colonial, about seventy-five years old. There are sheep, goats, ducks, geese and guinea fowl on the property, and guests may be welcomed by the Hirshes' friendly bluetick hounds. Everyone is invited to explore the estate's miles of grounds; a scenic, two-mile stretch of the Jackson River winds through the property and has been stocked with trout for fly-casting enthusiasts. Fort Dinwiddie, a frontier outpost built in 1754 and visited several times by George Washington, is within an easy walk. Tennis is available on the lodge's Dynaturf court, and you can golf on the renowned Cascades or Lower Cascades courses. Swimming, riding and skiing are also accessible nearby.

Guest accommodations include a first-floor suite with king-size bed, sitting room with sofa bed, fireplace and shared bath; a room with queen-size bed, sitting area and shared bath; and a suite and room above with a private bath. On the second floor are a suite with

Virginia & Washington D.C.

twin beds, a sitting room with sofa bed, private bath and screened porch, and a smaller suite with queen-size bed, private bath and screened porch. Also on the grounds, Craig's Cottage includes one bedroom with double bed and private bath and sitting room with sofa bed, kitchen and TV, and a second, larger bedroom with twin beds, a sitting area, fireplace, private bath and TV.

Meadow Lane's many amenities include a spacious Common Room with handsome antiques and two stone fireplaces, and the Breakfast Room, boasting a 1710 oak sideboard. A full breakfast, included in the rates, features various egg dishes: eggs Jackson are the house specialty. The Hirshes also own a small guest cottage in the Warm Springs Historic District. Francisco Cottage is a restored, enlarged 1820 log cabin, attractively furnished in antiques.

Meadow Lane Lodge, Star Route A, Box 110, Warm Springs, VA 24484; (703) 839-5959. (From Warm Springs, follow Rte. 39 west for 4 miles.) Rates are expensive, lower for longer stays. American Express, Visa and MasterCard are accepted. Children are welcome; no pets, please. Parking is available. Open April 1–Jan. 31.

Vine Cottage Inn. In Hot Springs, Wendell and Pat Lucas welcome guests to Vine Cottage Inn, a large Victorian house built in 1912. The inn is next door to the world-famous Homestead resort, and guests may use many of its facilities. Vine Cottage has eight bedrooms with private baths and six with semi-private baths for guests. Each inn room is decorated with a mixture of antique styles creating a "Country Charm" ambiance. Visitors are invited to relax in the living room with its brick fireplace, small library and TV, or sit out on the broad front porch and rock. Breakfast, which is included in the rates, consists of fresh fruit or juice, Pat's homemade rolls, and coffee or tea. Dinners are available at the inn on most nights with advance reservations.

Attractions in the area include the famed Hot Springs, 106-degree

Bed & Breakfast

baths in the Homestead Spa; excellent golfing; horseback and carriage riding; hiking, hunting and fishing; tennis and swimming. Skiing and skating are available at the Homestead in season. And north of town, the Bacova Guild shop offers lovely silk-screened gifts.

Vine Cottage Inn, P.O. Box 918, Hot Springs, VA 24445; (703) 839-2422. Rates are moderate; group rates on request. Visa, MasterCard and Choice are accepted. Children are welcome; pets may be allowed, but please ask first. Parking is available. Open year-round except for Dec. 24, 25 and 26.

Lynchburg

Lynchburg, southeast of Lexington, sits on seven hills overlooking the James River. Home of several schools, including Randolph-Macon Woman's College, Lynchburg was originally a tobacco town. During the Civil War, the city was a major storage depot and scene of a wartime battle. Six Confederate generals are buried here, including Gen. Jubal A. Early, who commanded the Southern forces during the brief Battle of Lynchburg.

Appomattox Court House, where Confederate Gen. Robert E. Lee surrendered to Gen. Ulysses S. Grant on April 9, 1865, ending the Civil War, is a short drive east of Lynchburg. The village, now a National Historic Park, has been restored and the Court House itself contains a museum and visitor center.

Sojourners. Sojourners, a comfortable bed-and-breakfast guest house in Lynchburg, is owned by Ann and Clyde McAlister. A contemporary brick ranch with a lower terrace level, the house is almost out of sight at the bottom of one of the town's many cul-de-sacs. The McAlisters have two rooms for travelers: one large bedroom with a double bed and a single bed with private bath, and a small single with shared bath. The first, an air-conditioned, heated, ground-level room, evolved from a carport and is now airy and bright, comfortably furnished with an easy chair, two small country pine tables, an old chest and a big wooden office desk. The bath area, which includes tub and shower, has a separate lavatory/vanity and walk-in closet, separated by louvered doors. The small bedroom features an unusual handmade chest and collectibles from childhood, including *St. Nicholas* magazines, fairytale books, wind-up toys and mugs.

Either a full or a continental breakfast is offered, included in the rates. The McAlisters make all their own bread, coffee cakes and buns. Guests are served in a small dining room which overlooks two acres of woodland, blooming with dogwood and redbud in the spring. In the fall, tulip poplars and sycamores add color, and as the leaves fall glimpses of the Blue Ridge Mountains appear. A window bird feeder attracts cardinals, chickadees, nuthatches, goldfinches and many other varieties of birdlife; deer occasionally wander through the backyard, and your hosts have even sighted a wild turkey.

Virginia & Washington D.C.

Visitors are encouraged to ramble through the grounds; there is a stream at the bottom of an incline, and a wealth of wildflowers. The property was once a park for a school that is now a private residence nearby. Hung throughout the house are landscape oil paintings by Ann's father, the late well-known North Carolina artist Robert P. Lawrence. Also on display are some interesting Oriental items and a few pieces of heirloom china. The friendly McAlisters, according to your hostess, have eclectic tastes and share a simple lifestyle. They enjoy sharing "their" mountains, woods and wildlife, as well as interests in genealogy, art and music with others of like interests. Guests are invited to share the family living room, books, games and TV.

Sojourners, 3609 Tanglewood Lane, Lynchburg, VA 24503; (804) 384-1655. (Advance reservations are required; when you write or phone, your hosts will send you a map with directions to the house.) Rates are moderate, discounted for more than 3 nights. Children under 12, $5 extra. (The single room is ideal for one child, and a crib is available.) No pets, please. Off-street parking is available. Smoking outside only. Open year-round.

Index

(Note: Listings preceded by * are reservation services.)

Alabama 13
Auburn, 19
    Crenshaw Guest House, 21
Birmingham, 19
    *Bed and Breakfast Birmingham, Inc., 19
Mentone, 15
    Mentone Inn, 16
Mobile, 22
    Vincent-Doan Home, 23
Scottsboro, 17
    Brunton House Bed and Breakfast, 17
    *Brunton's Bed and Breakfast, 18

Florida 25
Amelia Island, 26
    1735 House, 28
Fernandina Beach, 26
    Bailey House, 27
Key West, 35
    Coconut Grove Guest House, 37
    Curry House, 36
    Eaton Lodge, 36
Marathon, 40
    *Bed & Breakfast of the Florida Keys, Inc., 40
Miami, 40
    *Bed & Breakfast Co., 40
Palm Harbor, 40
    *Florida Suncoast Bed and Breakfast, 40
St. Augustine, 29
    Casa de Solana, 30
    Kenwood Inn, 32
    St. Francis Inn, 31
    Westcott House, 33

Bed & Breakfast

Sarasota, 38
    B & B By the Sea, 38
Tarpon Springs, 38
    Livery Stable, 39
Winter Park, 40
    *AAA Bed and Breakfast of Florida, Inc., 40

Georgia 41
Atlanta, 42
    Beverly Hills Inn, 42
Augusta, 48
    Telfair Inn, 48
Clarkesville, 47
    Charm House Inn, 47
Columbus, 51
    DeLoffre House, 51
Hoschton, 43
    Hillcrest Grove, 43
Lakemont, 44
    Lake Rabun Hotel, 44
Macon, 50
    Hutnick House, 50
Mountain City, 46
    York House, 46
Savannah, 52
    Ballastone Inn, 56
    Bed and Breakfast Inn, 61
    Charlton Court, 62
    Eliza Thompson House, 59
    "417" – Haslam-Fort House, 55
    Liberty Inn 1834, 58
    Morel House, 55
    Oglethorpe Inn, 61
Senoia, 49
    Culpepper House, 49
Statesboro, 52
    Statesboro Inn, 54

Louisiana 63
Baton Rouge, 66
    Mt. Hope Plantation Home and Gardens, 67
New Iberia, 66
    Mintmere Plantation, 70
New Orleans, 71
    Cornstalk Hotel, 76
    Hotel Maison de Ville, 74
    Lafitte Guest House, 73

Index

LaMothe House, 75
Soniat House, 77
Terrell House, 78
Ruston, 64
Twin Gables, 65
St. Francisville, 66
Cottage Plantation, 68

Mississippi 79

Holly Springs, 92
Hamilton Place, 92
Lorman, 80
Rosswood Plantation, 87
Natchez, 80
The Burn, 81
Elgin Plantation, 86
Linden, 85
Oakland Plantation, 87
Silver Street Inn, 83
Texada, 83
Port Gibson, 88
Oak Square, 90
Vicksburg, 88
Anchuca, 89

North Carolina 95

Asheville, 118
Flint Street Inn, 119
Old Reynolds Mansion, 121
Ray House Bed and Breakfast, 120
Blowing Rock, 116
Maple Lodge, 117
Boone, 115
Ole Waterloo, 116
Bryson City, 124
Folkestone Lodge, 125
Charlotte, 111
Blair-Bowden House, 112
Hampton Manor, 113
Homeplace, 113
Edenton, 101
Trestle House, 103
Franklin, 124
Buttonwood Inn, 126
Glenville, 124
Mountain High, 126

Bed & Breakfast

Greensboro, 105
    Greenwich, 108
    Greenwood, 107
Hendersonville, 118
    Reverie Bed and Breakfast, 122
Kill Devil Hills, 97
    Ye Olde Cherokee Inn, 99
Lake Lure, 118
    Lodge on Lake Lure, 122
New Bern, 101
    Harmony House Inn, 101
    Kings Arms, 101
Ocracoke, 97
    Beach House, 100
Pinehurst, 110
    Magnolia Inn, 110
Raleigh, 105
    Oakwood Inn, 106
Tryon, 118
    Mill Farm Inn, 123
Wilmington, 103
    Anderson Guest House, 103
    Murchison House, 104
Winston-Salem, 105
    Brookstown Inn Bed and Breakfast, 108
    Colonel Ludlow House, 109

South Carolina 129

Beaufort, 139
    Bay Street Inn, 139
    Thomas Rhett House Inn, 140
Charleston, 131
    Battery Carriage House, 135
    Elliott House Inn, 136
    Sword Gate Inn, 133
    Two Meeting Street Inn, 137
    Vendue Inn, 134

Tennessee 143

Knoxville, 147
    *Tennessee Southern Hospitality, Inc., 148
Memphis, 144
    Lowenstein-Long House, 144
Murfreesboro, 146
    Clardy's Guest House, 146
Rogersville, 149
    Hale Springs Inn, 149

Index

Virginia and Washington, D.C. 151
Charlottesville, 176
    Oxbridge Inn, 177
Chincoteague Island, 168
    Miss Molly's Inn, 168
    Year of the Horse Inn, 169
Hot Springs, 178
    Vine Cottage Inn, 181
Lexington, 178
    Mrs. Hunter McCormick/Guests, 179
    106 McDowell Street West, 179
Lynchburg, 182
    Sojourners, 182
Mathews, 161
    Riverfront House, 164
Middleburg, 171
    Welbourne, 172
Mt. Jackson, 170
    Widow Kip's Guest House, 170
Orange, 156
    Hidden Inn, 158
Richmond, 159
    Catlin-Abbott House, 160
Sperryville, 171
    Conyers House, 174
Upperville, 171
    1763 Inn, 171
Virginia Beach, 165
    Angie's Guest Cottage, 166
Warm Springs, 178
    Meadow Lane Lodge, 180
Washington, D.C., 152
    Kalorama Guest House-Kalorama Park, 154
    Kalorama Guest House-Woodley, 155
Williamsburg, 161
    *Williamsburg Inn Colonial Houses, 165

About the Author

Corinne Madden Ross, a free-lance writer who lives near Boston, stays in guest houses whenever possible on her many travels. She has published numerous travel articles and is author of **To Market, To Market: Six Walking Tours of the Old & the New Boston** (1980).

She is also the author of **The New England Bed and Breakfast Book** (East Woods Press, 1979) and the **The Mid-Atlantic Bed and Breakfast Book** (East Woods Press, 1983) and the co-author of **New England: Off the Beaten Path** (East Woods Press, 1981).

Pat Sabiston, who updated this edition of **Southern Bed and Breakfast**, is a writer who specializes in non-fiction projects. She lives in Albany, Georgia.

East Woods Press Books

Backcountry Cooking
Berkshire Trails for Walking & Ski Touring
Best Bed & Breakfast in the World, The
California Bed & Breakfast
Campfire Chillers
Campfire Songs
Canoeing the Jersey Pine Barrens
Carolina Curiosities
Carolina Seashells
Carpentry: Some Tricks of the Trade from an Old-Style Carpenter
Catfish Cookbook, The
Charlotte: A Touch of Gold
Complete Guide to Backpacking in Canada
Day Trips From Cincinnati
Day Trips From Houston
Drafting: Tips and Tricks on Drawing and Designing House Plans
Fructose Cookbook, The
Grand Strand: An Uncommon Guide to Myrtle Beach, The
Healthy Trail Food Book, The
Hiking from Inn to Inn
Hiking Virginia's National Forests
Historic Country House Hotels
How to Play with Your Baby
Interior Finish: More Tricks of the Trade
Just Folks: Visitin' with Carolina People
Kays Gary, Columnist
Maine Coast: A Nature Lover's Guide, The
Mid-Atlantic Guest House Book, The
New England Bed and Breakfast Book, The
New England: Off the Beaten Path
Ohio: Off the Beaten Path
Parent Power!
Race, Rock and Religion
Rocky Mountain National Park Hiking Trails
Saturday Notebook, The
South Carolina Hiking Trails
Southern Bed and Breakfast Book, The
Southern Rock: A Climber's Guide to the South
Sweets Without Guilt
Tar Heel Sights: Guide to North Carolina's Heritage
Tennessee Trails
Train Trips: Exploring America by Rail
Trout Fishing the Southern Appalachians
Vacationer's Guide to Orlando and Central Florida, A
Walks in the Catskills
Walks in the Great Smokies
Walks with Nature in Rocky Mountain National Park
Whitewater Rafting in Eastern America
Woman's Journey, A
You Can't Live on Radishes

Available from bookstores or from:
The East Woods Press
429 East Boulevard
Charlotte, NC 28203
(704) 334-0897